T0318949

Cambridge Elements

Elements in Histories of Emotions and the Senses
edited by
Jan Plamper
Goldsmiths, University of London

NEWBORN IMITATION

The Stakes of a Controversy

Ruth Leys
Johns Hopkins University

CAMBRIDGE
UNIVERSITY PRESS

University Printing House, Cambridge CB2 8BS, United Kingdom

One Liberty Plaza, 20th Floor, New York, NY 10006, USA

477 Williamstown Road, Port Melbourne, VIC 3207, Australia

314–321, 3rd Floor, Plot 3, Splendor Forum, Jasola District Centre,
New Delhi – 110025, India

79 Anson Road, #06–04/06, Singapore 079906

Cambridge University Press is part of the University of Cambridge.

It furthers the University's mission by disseminating knowledge in the pursuit of education, learning, and research at the highest international levels of excellence.

www.cambridge.org
Information on this title: www.cambridge.org/9781108826730
DOI: 10.1017/9781108920308

First published 2020

A catalogue record for this publication is available from the British Library.

ISBN 978-1-108-82673-0 (paperback)
ISSN 2632-1068 (online)
ISSN 2632-105X (print)

Newborn Imitation

The Stakes of a Controversy

Elements in Histories of Emotions and the Senses

DOI: 10.1017/9781108920308
First published online: July 2020

Ruth Leys
Johns Hopkins University

Author for correspondence: Ruth Leys, leys100@gmail.com

Abstract: Newborn imitation has recently become the focus of a major controversy in the human sciences. New studies have reexamined the evidence and found it wanting. Imitation has been regarded as a crucial capability of neonates ever since 1977, when two American psychologists first published experiments appearing to demonstrate that babies are able to copy a variety of facial movements at birth. The findings overturned decades of assumptions about the competence of newborns. But what if claims for newborn imitation are not true? Influential theories about the mechanisms underlying imitation, the role of mirror neurons, the nature of the self and infant mental states will all have to be modified or abandoned if it turns out that babies cannot imitate at birth. This Element offers a critical assessment of those theories and the stakes involved.

Keywords: Imitation, Newborn

ISBNs: 9781108826730 (PB), 9781108920308 (OC)
ISSNs: 2632-1068 (online), 2632-105X (print)

Contents

> Neonatal imitation, or the capacity of newborns to flexibly copy others' actions … is one of the most controversial purported phenomena in all of psychological science.[1]

1 Introduction

This is an account of the vicissitudes of theories associated with the idea of newborn imitation. Since 1977, when two American psychologists, Andrew N. Meltzoff and M. Keith Moore, published the results of their first experiments on the topic, the claim that babies can imitate certain facial and other movements at birth has become a core assumption of most accounts of neonatal behavior (Meltzoff & Moore 1977). Although some scientists had doubts, their criticisms were lost amid the general enthusiasm that greeted findings suggesting that neonates could undertake the complex task of copying specific movements, such as protruding the tongue and facial-emotional expressions.

New studies, however, have reexamined the data and found them wanting. In particular, a comprehensive longitudinal study of newborn imitation by Oostenbroek and her colleagues, published in 2016, found no evidence for it, with the result that the validity of the original claims have yet again been contested (Oostenbroek et al. 2016). According to these researchers, past findings have largely been an artifact of poorly controlled experimental conditions. Their conclusions have rekindled the debate between believers and skeptics on the issue of newborn imitation, and the course of the controversy shows no clear path toward resolution.

What is the dispute about? In important ways, the debate is about more than just neonatal imitation. We are witnessing unprecedented levels of scrutiny of previously "iconic" experiments at a time when worries about replicability and validity are tainting the psychological and social sciences (Zwan et al. 2018; Morawski 2019). The clash over the integrity of previous findings on newborn imitation belongs to this development. The details of the debate over methodology, control procedures, the role of publication bias, and related issues are clearly important. But what interests me is less the question of the solidity of the evidence favoring claims about neonatal imitation than the theoretical ideas about infant development that have been built on those claims. As Oostenbroek et al. have remarked, if their experimental findings and arguments hold up, then "the many prominent theories built upon the assumption of neonatal imitation … are not empirically supported and should be modified or abandoned altogether" (Oostenbroek et al. 2016, 1336).[2]

[1] Davis et al. 2020, quoted by permission.

[2] The publication of this paper precipitated a number of exchanges and responses. See Meltzoff et al. 2018; Oostenbroek et al. 2018; Meltzoff et al. 2019; Davis et al. 2020; Redshaw et al. 2020. For

Oostenbroek et al. do not identify what prominent theories would require revision or rejection should neonatal imitation be disproven, but their remark indicates the important stakes that attend the outcome. These are what I plan to discuss. It will be impossible to do full justice to all the relevant issues, but I believe it will be useful to assemble in one analysis the various ramifications of the debate. By doing so, my aim is to provide a starting point for a larger history of the vicissitudes of the idea of newborn imitation.

2 Piaget Before Meltzoff and Moore

Participants in contemporary research on newborn imitation generally consider the topic to have been shaped by the founding work of the Swiss psychologist Jean Piaget (1896–1980). In the 1970s, before the impact of Meltzoff and Moore's decisive intervention, Piaget's widely influential studies of development in childhood had already become the focus of considerable scrutiny among American psychologists. His theoretical analyses and conclusions were being reassessed, and his empirical claims reexamined by ostensibly more rigorous experimental techniques than the more naturalistic and "anecdotal" methods he had used when studying individual children (Kaplan 1971, xv–xvi; Costall & Leudar 2004).

In discussions of Piaget's work in the early 1970s, when his reputation among American psychologists was at its height, commentators focused as much on Piaget's contributions to epistemology as on his empirical findings. The topic of infant imitation, which Piaget had investigated so carefully and whose development he had made central to the infant's ability to construct its understanding of the world, tended to be mentioned only in passing (Kessen 1996, 196–99). The reception of his work in the 1970s in the USA belonged to a moment when the dominance of behaviorism was being challenged by a cognitive revolution that once again placed the human mind at the center of the psychological sciences. The premise that the tenets of behaviorism and learning theory were sufficient to explain all cognitive development gave way to the idea that more attention needed to be paid to the relations between the child's mental structures and its environment. Authors recognized that Piaget had placed that question at the center of his approach to psychology, an approach he had labeled "genetic epistemology" (Piaget 1953; 1954; 1962; 1972; Piaget & Inhelder 1969).

It was understood precisely in this connection that Piaget had attempted to steer a careful middle course between, as he conceived it, the extremes of

further contributions to the dispute see also Ray & Heyes 2011; Oostenbroek et al. 2013; Suddendorf et al. 2013; Simpson et al. 2014; Jones 2016; 2017; Kennedy-Constantini et al. 2017; Keven & Akins 2017; Meltzoff 2017; Vincini et al. 2017b.

idealism (or rationalism, or what he called "preformationism") on the one hand and empiricism on the other. Idealism, associated with the work of Kant and also Gestalt psychology, was seen by him as rightly stressing the role of cognitive structures or laws in mental development, but as neglecting the importance of individual experience. In contrast, he saw empiricism as properly emphasizing the contingencies of individual life but as disregarding the framework of the subject's cognitive "schemas" within which, he held, mentation and intelligence were constructed. Thus, Piaget's program in psychology stressed the roles of adaptation, homeostasis, assimilation, and autoregulation as biological and behavioral processes that mediated the relationship between the organism's schemas of action and its exchanges with the environment at different stages in the development of cognition and knowledge.

Piaget's contributions to genetic epistemology raised an important question. Had he achieved the right balance in his neo-Kantian or "dynamic" account of the relations between his postulated basic sensorimotor action programs or later cognitive schemas and the products of experience? The question became weightier when, influenced in part by Noam Chomsky's contemporaneous assertions concerning the importance of genetically determined, universal grammatical structures in the acquisition of language competence (e.g., Chomsky 1968), commentators in the 1970s began to give increased attention to the role of innate cognitive organization and capacities in the child's mental development.

The question of the respective merits of innatism versus constructivism in the origin of human mentation, especially the origin of human linguistic capacity, stimulated a highly informative debate between Piaget and Chomsky at a conference in 1975 (Piattelli-Palmarini 1980). More generally, we can say that this was a moment in American psychology when the previous hostility to biological explanations in psychology, based on the rejection of Nazi racism, gave way to a more general universalist and evolutionary-biological approach to human behavior. Chomsky's postwar development of a theory of a universal grammar, the 1960s and 1970s rise of an evolutionary "affect program" approach to the emotions associated with the work of Silvan Tomkins and Paul Ekman (more on this in a moment), and the enthusiastic reception of Meltzoff and Moore's claims for the innate imitative capacities of the newborn all belong to this development.

An important issue in this connection was whether Piaget had given a valid account of how infants and children acquire knowledge of objects and the world, especially how they form concepts (Bellin 1971, 86). Piaget had offered a complex picture of infant development in this regard. Among his pivotal insights was the claim that in infancy the development of concepts or the "categories of reason" develop over time in a series of universal but discontinuous stages. Each stage was marked by specific, progressively more elaborate, cognitive schemas as the child constructs its knowledge of the world, with this knowledge in turn based on the interaction between its biological maturation and its perceptions of the environment.

For example, according to Piaget, in the first, "sensorimotor stage" of development, infants lack the mental representations of the world necessary for understanding object permanence. He demonstrated this empirically by showing that, at first, babies cannot appreciate that an object still exists when it is hidden from view. He therefore suggested that they do not possess the concept of an object and hence a true conception of physical reality, space, substance, and causal relations (Bellin 1971, 100). Piaget suggested that it is not until the ninth or tenth month that the child actively searches for vanished objects by removing materials that obscure them or hinder the child from reaching for them. According to Piaget, the infant's initial understanding of the physical world is thus qualitatively different from that of the adult. The task of his research was to identify those differences.

Piaget's discussions of the origin of concepts led investigators in several directions. In one direction, his arguments led to philosophical inquiries regarding the long-standing question of the nature of perception itself. Here, the key issue was whether perception was best thought of as inherently conceptual or whether it could be conceived as processing "stimuli" in the absence of conceptual knowledge. The philosopher David Hamlyn, in a 1971 commentary on Piaget, weighed in on the conceptualist side in Wittgensteinian terms not unlike those subsequently expressed forcefully and influentially by the philosopher John McDowell (Hamlyn 1971; 1978; Russell 1979; McDowell 1996). But Meltzoff and Moore's claims for the capacity of newborns to imitate suggested that they possessed a perceptual-cognitive capability which preceded the acquisition of language and concepts. As we shall see, that is why, in the wake of such claims, several philosophers already committed to the idea of nonconceptual content in perception came to buttress their arguments by appealing to the findings of neonatal imitation.

In a more empirical direction, researchers questioned whether Piaget was right to suggest – as had Freud before him – that infants are born into an undifferentiated world of "blooming, buzzing confusion," as William James had described it (James 1890, 488), in which at first they perceive no distinction between themselves and their environment. As the British developmental psychologist George Butterworth wrote in a volume of essays on the topic of Piaget's epistemology: "Piaget's account of the developmental dependencies between perceiving, acting, and knowing is based on the premise that the initial relation between infant and environment is one of profound adualism … According to Piaget there is no information in the structure of stimulation itself that will allow response contingent feedback to be distinguished from independent sensory data" (Butterworth 1982, 137). For Piaget, it is a developmental achievement when the child succeeds in understanding the separation between itself and others, and hence in differentiating its subjective experiences from an independent, objective reality.

That this self–world boundary was acquired, however, was antithetical to the position taken by Meltzoff and Moore. They proposed that from the start the newborn possesses the cognitive capacity to discriminate perceptually the borders between itself and other persons and objects, and can thus distinguish self and nonself. Their findings raised the following question: Is the newborn as "incompetent" and "un-adapted" to the concrete world of people and objects as Piaget had proposed? Or is the infant pre-equipped to a far greater degree than Piaget had realized? (Russell 1982, 19).

Such questions inspired a flurry of experimental work on infant perception. Hamlyn suggested that the issues raised by Piaget's discussions of perceptual development were inherently philosophical and conceptual, so empirical investigations alone could not resolve the epistemological issues at stake. However, his suggestions did not deter the numerous researchers who embarked on detailed experimental studies of infant development at this time. An influential figure in this regard was the psychologist James Gibson, who rejected the perceptual constructivism central to Piaget's views and instead, in his book *The Senses Considered as Perceptual Systems* (1966) and subsequent publications, proposed that the organism directly perceives or picks up "information" in the ambient visual array. According to Gibson, perception is not governed by internal, computational representations in the mind-brain, as cognitive scientists tended to argue, but stems directly from the stimulus. Nor does learning occur through a constructivist-conceptualizing process, as Piaget had suggested. Rather, it occurs through the infant's increasing ability to extract information immediately from the environment by differentiating among properties and recognizing distinctive features. Those properties inhere in the environment itself, providing what Gibson came to call "affordances" to the developing organism (Gibson 1966, 2; see also Gibson 1986).

Exactly what Gibson meant by "information" and the notion of "affordance" has implications for the theoretical issues raised by claims about neonatal imitation. The relevant questions include whether (a) he successfully challenged cognitivist theories positing "inner representations" or information-processing functions mediating between the organism and the world, or instead succumbed to those same cognitivist theories; and (b), as he argued against

Kant, there is no need for references to "conception and belief" in immediate human perception. For the moment, though, it suffices to note that Gibson's views were attractive to those involved in challenging Piaget's ideas. Thus, based on both Gibson's views and Meltzoff and Moore's claims for inborn imitative skills, Butterworth assigned to the neonate a "pre-reflexive" level of sensory and perceptual awareness that "precedes the acquisition of self-conscious concepts and beliefs" (Butterworth 1982, 139). The implication was that infants possess the ability to make certain discriminations and judgments at the very start of life, without the need for learning – or indeed for any concepts at all. Similarly, and influentially, in *Varieties of Reference*, also published in 1982, the philosopher Gareth Evans cited Gibson's work when defending the claim that the content of perception is nonconceptual – more on this later (Evans 1982, 122–23).

Another important figure, especially in the field of infant development, was Gibson's wife, Eleanor Gibson, who at Cornell University pioneered the study of perception and perceptual learning in a variety of animals, including human infants. She adopted the same views concerning direct perception as her husband, and her work soon became a magnet for a cohort of talented younger psychologists committed to contributing to the field of infant development. They included Elizabeth Spelke (probably her best-known student) and Tom Bower, whose experiments and ideas, as we shall see, would play a crucial role in Meltzoff and Moore's attempts to explain newborn imitation (Gibson 1969, 13–14).[3]

3 The Primordial Unity of the Senses

A key topic in the study of perception has been whether, as most psychologists have assumed, the different sensory modalities are originally distinct, such that "intermodal" connections or "transfers" require later learning and integration. Or might the reverse be true? Are we instead born with a primordial unity of the senses, a unity that must differentiate during individual development for us to have distinct modalities?

An important moment in the long history of discussion of this topic was when the seventeenth-century Irish writer William Molyneux posed a famous question to the philosopher John Locke: Will a man born blind and taught by touch to discriminate between a cube and a sphere of metal be able by sight alone, if his eyesight were to be restored in adulthood, to tell the difference between the two

[3] For Eleanor Gibson's well known "visual cliff" experiments appearing to show depth perception in non-human animals and human infants alike see Gibson & Walk 1960; Sorce et al. 1985; Rodkey 2015; Burman 2017.

shapes? Molyneux's answer was No, because the man would not have had the necessary prior experience of associating touch with sight. In other words, Molyneux held that the unity or integration of the senses was a product of learning and experience. Piaget agreed that the sensory modalities are at first separate and only become integrated with experience and the development of the relevant schemas (Gibson 1969, 230; see also Piaget & Inhelder 1969, 15; Morgan 1977).

Since Molyneux's query, various reports had appeared of the perceptual experiences of congenitally blind individuals whose sight had been restored in adulthood, with mixed conclusions. The topic interested both William James and Eleanor Gibson. As she observed, in the 1930s and onwards several authors had adopted the opposite position from that of Molyneux by arguing instead for the "unity of the senses," or what the Belgian psychologist Albert Michotte, in his influential studies of perception, called "amodal perception." By amodal perception Michotte meant the perception of information that is common or redundant across multiple senses (the phenomenon of synesthesia is an instance of this). As Gibson recounted, Michotte and his students demonstrated that subjects reported perceiving visual details that did not correspond to actual sensations but were instead a product of the total perceptual situation (Gibson cited Michotte et al. 1964). An example of this is what happens when discontinuities in the perception of a scene, due to the retinal blind-spot, are nevertheless filled in and the discontinuities ignored. Gibson accepted the phenomenon of amodal perception, though not Michotte's explanation of the phenomenon. This is because she believed that, according to James Gibson's perceptual theory, all the necessary information was already present in the visual field. As she remarked:

> I shall borrow Michotte's term amodal, though not his interpretation of amodal perception. I mean the term to suggest that there is information in stimulation which is not tied to specific sensations but is rather invariant over them. Many distinctive features of objects and events are of this kind (corners, motions, temporal patterns, and transitions). Information for them may be extracted from more than one kind of sensory experience. Perhaps all cross-modal similarity is really amodal in this sense. In that case might not cross-modal transfer be explained on the basis of amodal identities, higher order properties of stimulation which are not sensation specific? (Gibson 1969, 219)

Gibson answered this question in the affirmative when she concluded: "The integration of originally separate [sensory] systems is not the way of development; it seems more likely that the systems did not originate as independent single channels; and that independence is a learned achievement rather than an interdependence" (Gibson 1969, 381).

The idea of the original unity of the senses and their subsequent differentiation in development was taken up and elaborated by Tom Bower, under the rubric "*supramodal*" perception. On the basis of his findings in numerous experiments on perception in young infants, Bower became convinced that the traditional view that sensory integration requires time and learning was incorrect. Infants as young as two weeks, he suggested, exhibited "marked distress" as measured by their surprise response when they perceived an approaching object. In his view, the finding of distress in such immature infants contradicted the theory that the perception of the solidity of objects was learned or constructed by associating tactile impressions and vision; hence, he concluded that the perception of the solidity of objects occurred in newborns. Bower was perhaps hasty when he inferred, from the signs of alarm in such a young baby at an approaching solid object, that it perceived and was therefore afraid of the impingement of a solid mass on its body, but this is the inference he made. On the basis of these and related considerations, he therefore suggested that vision and touch are coordinated in a unity at birth (Bower 1971, 32–33; see also Bower et al. 1970b, 51–53).

In a 1974 book on infant development, Bower named the system governing this primitive unity of the senses the *supramodal system*, defined as a system capable of discerning the properties of objects that can be specified via any sensory modality (Bower 1974a, 121). And in a paper that same year, he made the case for the evolutionary origins of the supramodal system, citing several studies apparently demonstrating the existence of auditory-visual and tactile-visual coordination in neonates (Bower 1974b, 151). I note that the debate between nativists, who, like Gibson and Bower, believe that infants are born with a unified sensory system that only becomes differentiated in development, versus the empiricists, who judge that life begins with differentiated sensory systems that are only integrated over time, has yet to be resolved. But I think it is fair to say that the preponderance of the available evidence favors the empiricist position, not the nativist one.[4]

[4] It is a sign of the reach of Meltzoff's claims about neonatal imitation that at the very start of their influential book, *The Merging of the Senses* (1993), authors Barry Stein and M. Alex Meredith observed, with reference to claims for the existence of neonatal imitation and the nativist position, that "whether newborns are already capable of apprehending unique qualities in different senses or actually perceive all senses as the same remain open questions." They reproduced Meltzoff's striking images showing 2- to 3-week-old babies ostensibly matching an adult's modeling of certain facial movements (see Figure 1), but observed that there was no current support for Bower's and others' view that the different sensory modalities have evolved from an undifferentiated and therefore "supramodal" primordial system (Stein & Meredith 1993, x, 11–15, 21; see also Calvert et al. 2004). In a more recent publication, Stein and his coauthors again mention the behavioral evidence of neonatal imitation as showing that newborns can detect certain cross-modal correspondences in very early life. However, they go on to state that research on the

Curiously, in a hitherto unremarked paper of 1976, a year before Meltzoff and Moore reported their findings about newborn imitation, Bower published photographs showing a six-day-old baby, in the arms of its mother, imitating the protrusion of the mother's tongue.[5] Bower treated the imitation as a significant example of the functioning of certain sensorimotor skills at birth, observing that:

> In the area of sensory-motor coordination … one must include the fact that newborn infants show an extraordinary capacity for imitating the behavior of an adult. For example, they are quite able to imitate an adult sticking out his tongue, opening his mouth, or widening his eyes. Indeed, this ability is the most remarkable example known of the competence of the newborn's perceptual system.

He went on to remark:

> Consider what is involved in imitating someone's sticking out his tongue. The infant must identify the thing he sees in the adult's mouth as being a tongue … He must realize that the thing he cannot see but can feel in his own mouth is also a tongue … He must then execute fairly complex muscular movements in order to imitate what he sees. (Bower 1976, 38)

In other words, the newborn seemed capable of performing opaque or "non-visible" imitations, so-called because they are movements the baby makes in order to match its own proprioceptive sensations when moving its tongue (movements that it can feel but not see because it has yet to see its face in a mirror), with the movements of the tongue of an adult (movements that it can see but not feel).[6]

This imitative skill seemed extraordinary to Bower since it apparently required highly specific mapping between the visual and the proprioceptive systems. At first, he believed it was incompatible with his theory that perception starts with more abstract, unified supramodal responses and proceeds over time toward more differentiated sensory reactions (he would later change his mind about this; Bower 1978, 93; 1989a, 90–99; 1989b, 31–32). But Meltzoff and Moore had no such qualms: they seized on Bower's idea of an innate

physiology of the development of cross-modal sensory integration in the superior colliculus of the newborn cat, the principal source of what is known on this topic, demonstrates that the capacity to integrate information across senses is not an inherent feature of the newborn's brain, but develops in "an experience-dependent manner during early postnatal life" (Stein et al. 2014, 521).

[5] See also Jane Dunkeld's studies of infant imitation during the 1970s, undertaken at the direction of Bower (Dunkeld 1978). Dunkeld is credited with the photograph of neonatal imitation in Bower 1976 (see Bower 1977, 29).

[6] For the term "non-visible" for newborn imitation, see Moore & Meltzoff 1978, 153.

"supramodal" perceptual capacity in order to explain their finding that newborns are able to imitate adult movements.

4 The Discovery of Newborn Imitation

Meltzoff and Moore's announcement in 1977 that neonates are able to imitate certain facial and other movements in adults was hailed as revolutionary by many American psychologists (Meltzoff & Moore 1977).[7] It was considered astonishing that newborns could produce such complex movements at the very start of life (Trevarthen et al. 1999, 128; see also Bower 1989b, 18). The phenomenon of imitation had been viewed as dependent on cognitive abilities that Piaget and others had deemed beyond the capacity of newborns. For Piaget, infants only develop the sensorimotor and cognitive skills necessary to achieve imitative matching at a later stage of development. Meltzoff and Moore deliberately threw down the gauntlet by confidently asserting that their experimental results disproved Piaget's views: "The experiments we report show that the infant's imitative competence has been underestimated. We find that 12- to 21-day-old infants can imitate both facial and manual gestures. This result has implications for our conception of innate human abilities and for theories of social and cognitive development" (Meltzoff & Moore 1977, 75).

Meltzoff and Moore's experiments have been described so often that only the barest account of them is necessary here. In their first published experiment they tested the ability of six alert 12- to 21-day-old infants to copy four movements performed by an experimenter standing in front of them: tongue protrusion, mouth opening, lip protrusion, and a sequential finger movement (opening and closing the hand by serially moving the fingers). The experiment was undertaken specifically to assess Piaget's claims for the late development of imitation in childhood. Each gesture was demonstrated four times in a 15-second stimulus presentation period, followed by a 20-second response period when the experimenter assumed a passive face. The infants' responses were videotaped and scored in a random order by undergraduate volunteers who were asked to determine which facial gesture they thought the infant was most likely imitating in each recorded infant response. In the case of the hand movements, the coders were asked to assess which of four hand movements, including the sequential finger movements, they thought the infants were responding to.

[7] The authors quickly published several more studies in which they announced their challenge to Piaget. As far as I am aware, the first published reference to Meltzoff and Moore's findings is in Parton 1976, based on Moore & Meltzoff 1975. Meltzoff and Moore's 1977 observations of early imitation was in fact preceded by some similar reports, including the following: Gardner & Gardner 1970; Maratos 1973.

To rule out the possibility that the experimenter was unintentionally prefiltering or shaping the data by re-administering the stimulus presentations in ways that made them coincide with the behavior being modeled, a second study was designed to avoid this potential confound. Moreover, apparently in order to meet an anticipated objection that arousal alone could explain the results, Meltzoff and Moore introduced a "differential imitation" procedure. This involved testing whether a specific imitation was evoked more frequently by the corresponding movement than by other modelled movements (i.e., infants should produce more mouth openings to modelled mouth opening than to tongue protrusion, lip protrusion, or any finger movements) (Meltzoff 1988; Butterworth 1999a, 71; Vincini et al. 2017a, 2–4). The evidence appeared to validate their claim that newborns possessed an innate capacity to imitate adult facial and other displays. In subsequent experiments, Meltzoff and Moore also appeared to demonstrate that older infants could imitate a simple action both immediately and after a 24-hour delay, suggesting that infants could not only recognize a current scene but remember that specific scene and reproduce the associated movement later (Meltzoff 1985a). The terms "early imitation" or "neonatal imitation" now commonly designate imitation that occurs in the first two months of life (Vincini & Jhang 2018, 397).[8]

Skepticism arose in some quarters about Meltzoff and Moore's findings, and efforts to replicate them sometimes failed.[9] Nevertheless, Meltzoff and Moore's results were seized on with alacrity by many developmental psychologists and lay persons alike. The positive reaction owed something to the efficacy of the images that accompanied Meltzoff and Moore's 1977 paper (see Figure 1). The pictures of the infant's imitations, paired with images of the experimenter presenting identically, made the matches appear precise and unquestionable, though it was unclear whether the images had been cherry-picked or arranged for dramatic effect. But this alone does not explain the groundswell of enthusiasm accorded Meltzoff and Moore's claims. It's as if the moment was ripe for a finding that appeared to overthrow decades of Piagetian assumptions about the minimal competence of the newborn. In line with Eleanor Gibson's and Bower's previous work, Meltzoff and Moore's results suggested that infants at birth possessed far greater cognitive capacities than those posited by Piaget. As Hayes and Watson commented in a critique of the new claims, the evidence of neonatal imitation seemed to provide "exemplary support for the exciting new notion that infants possess heretofore unexpected cognitive perceptual competence" (Hayes & Watson 1981, 657, 659).

[8] For Meltzoff and Moore's explanation for the drop out of facial imitation in the 2–3-month age range, see Meltzoff & Moore 1992.

[9] The literature on neonatal imitation is vast. For critical overviews of the experimental findings, see Oostenbroek et al. 2016; Jones 2009; 2017.

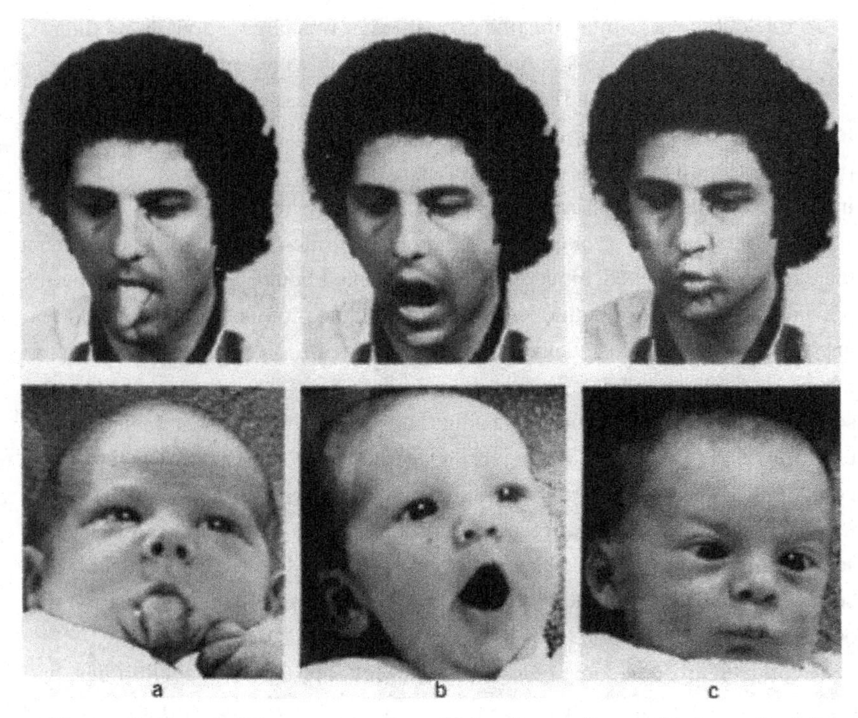

Figure 1. Sample Photographs from Video-Recordings of 2–3-week-old Infants Imitating Facial Movements Demonstrated by an Adult Experimenter. From Andrew N. Meltzoff & M. Keith Moore. (1977). Imitation of Facial and Manual Gestures by Human Neonates. *Science, New Series, 198 (4312), 75.* Reproduced by permission.

Meltzoff and Moore have built their careers on their neonatal imitation findings, refining and varying their experiments on newborns, studying response capacities as infants mature, rebutting criticisms, and repeating and elaborating their theoretical explanations. In 1982, Field et al. published the results of experiments allegedly demonstrating that neonates were capable of imitating certain "facial expressions of emotions." In framing their study, Field et al. relied on methods and assumptions adopted in earlier studies, chiefly by Tomkins and McCarter (1964) and Ekman and Friesen (1971). In those studies, the authors claimed to have demonstrated the existence of a small number of universal, evolved, genetically hardwired, reflex-like "primary affects" or "basic emotions" governed by subcortical "affect programs" in the brain. According to Tomkins and Ekman, each discrete affect or emotion triggers distinct physiological and behavioral patterns of response, most conspicuously the involuntary production of characteristic pan-cultural facial expressions that are automatically recognized by others. The list of "basic emotions" varied, but usually included a minimum of six affects, including happiness, sadness, anger, fear, surprise, and disgust.

In their experiments, Tomkins and McCarter, and later Ekman and Friesen, used still photographs of adults posing facial expressions that supposedly epitomized the discrete emotions. The photographs were employed as stimuli in tasks requiring Americans (Tomkins and McCarter) and members of various non-Western cultures, including the preliterate Fore peoples of New Guinea (Ekman and Friesen), to match posed expressions to emotion terms or stories. Field et al. adopted a related testing strategy, founded on this basic emotion paradigm, by asking two adult models to pose putative happy, sad, and surprised expressions in front of 74 newborns (median age 36 hours). The model held the baby upright and facing her, with the newborn's head supported with one hand and its body in the other; the model's and baby's faces were separated by approximately 10 inches. The baby's facial movements were coded by an observer, who stood behind the model and could see the infant's face, but was unaware of which expression the model was posing. Split-screen videotapes of the baby's and model's faces were made in order to allow reliability checks on the observer's coding and the model's facial presentations.

The published paper reproduced the observer's coding results and guesses as to which expression was being copied, along with six videotape images showing close matches between the facial expressions of the model and infant, although it is unclear whether the pictures were cherry-picked. Altogether, the results seemed to offer compelling evidence that newborns could faithfully copy the model's different facial expressions. The researchers therefore presented their experiments as further support for Meltzoff and Moore's claims for neonatal imitation. In 1983, using the same methods, Field et al. reported similar results with preterm neonates (Field et al. 1982; 1983; 1986).[10] Their findings were quickly incorporated into the newborn imitation literature.

According to the logic of the basic emotion paradigm, Field et al.'s results suggested that when infants matched the model's specific facial expressions, they also experienced the emotional states held to produce them. It does not seem to have occurred to the researchers that the babies might have been merely copying the model's facial movements without actually feeling or empathizing with the emotion apparently signified by the model's faces. Thus, in their paper

[10] For the "primary affects" or "basic emotions" papers cited by Field et al., see Tomkins & McCarter 1964 and Ekman & Friesen 1971.

Field et al. stated that they were studying "facial expressions of emotions" which, "because of their early appearance and their apparent universality … may reflect innate processes" (Field et al. 1982, 179). The dilemma presented by Field et al.'s research but unacknowledged by them – and, indeed, by most neonatal imitation researchers – was that there might be a disjunction between the infant's facial imitations and its emotional states. But if Field et al.'s infants were only duplicating the movements of "emotional expressions" without experiencing the emotions themselves, then by the logic of the basic emotion paradigm the babies were engaging in neonatal deception, and deception, according to Tomkins and Ekman required learning via socialization.[11]

Moreover, although Field et al. aimed to test whether the supposedly innate "facial expressions of emotions" could be easily copied, their experimental design could not determine whether those faces were indeed privileged. At a minimum, the researchers should have asked their models to pose "nonsense" faces as well as putatively happy, sad, and surprise ones, in order to determine whether infant's mimetic abilities were confined to certain "emotional expressions," as the researchers believed, or whether they extended to a range of facial behaviors outside their theoretical assumptions.[12]

More generally, the entire basis of the Field et al, study was flawed, because the authors presupposed Tomkins' and Ekman's claim for the existence of close connections between certain facial behaviors and the basic emotions, a claim that has been definitively challenged by Alan Fridlund, James Russell, and others. In 1994, both Fridlund and Russell demolished key empirical findings repeatedly cited as confirming Ekman's position (Fridlund 1994; 2017; Russell, 1994; see also Leys 2007, 2017). Fridlund also dismantled Ekman's experiments and his theoretical arguments concerning an assumed distinction between two kinds of facial expressions: the supposedly authentic expressions we exhibit in private when no one is watching, and the deceptive or "false" expressions we display in public in order to conform to cultural expectations and conventions. Fridlund rejected this distinction as incoherent and unsustainable (Fridlund 1994; see also Fridlund 2017; Leys 2017). Moreover, in contradiction of the basic emotion theory, recent findings of cultural diversity in facial displays indicate that mechanisms other than the evolutionary-phylogenetic ones posited by Tomkins and Ekman may well be in play, suggesting a role for cultural selection

[11] The question of whether the infants imitating the models' faces themselves experienced the emotions ostensibly underlying them, or could have been dissimulating, might well have been asked of the models too.

[12] For a failure to replicate Field et al.'s studies, see Kaitz et al. 1988. For criticisms of the Field et al. studies see Nelson 1987; Poulson et al. 1989, 290; Anisfeld 1991, 76–77, 84–87; Ruba & Repacholi 2019.

and transmission. This would likely entail imitation as one way whereby the child learns the culture's modes of social interaction.[13]

In the 1980s, however, the inadequacies of Tomkins's and Ekman's views were not evident to most researchers. Field et al.'s findings therefore seemed plausible and were quickly accepted by many scientists studying neonatal imitation. More troubling is the persistence of interest in these experiments despite the subsequent dismantling of their "basic emotion" premises. One reason for the continued citation of Field et al.'s studies is that many researchers remain committed to the basic emotion theory and to the idea that the perception of emotions in others is innate, with the result that they find Field et al.'s results convenient.

Meltzoff and Moore's findings, the results obtained by Field et al., and related experiments by other researchers led to the belief that neonatal imitation was a crucial component in the development of social cognition. Meltzoff and Moore suggested that at least some of the knowledge required for newborn imitation was acquired through associative learning while the baby was in the womb (Meltzoff & Moore 1977), although, as Jones has recently pointed out, this learning would account for only a small part of the knowledge the newborn would need in order to perform opaque imitations (Jones 2016). Accordingly, in Meltzoff and Moore's work, the emphasis fell on the existence of an inherited imitative competence and knowledge at birth. That newborns could imitate facial and other movements was also viewed as a precursor to the kinds of unconscious mimicry observed in adults who copy others without being aware of doing so, thus contributing to the rise of "priming" studies. And in the neuroscience push of the 1990s, neonatal imitation became closely linked to research on mirror neurons and attempts to relate them to embodied intersubjectivity, self-awareness, and emotional empathy, first in primates and then in humans. In short, despite some replication failures and validity concerns about the evidence, neonatal imitation became the cornerstone of most accounts of human development, social learning, and cultural evolution.

It is important to note that, according to Meltzoff and Moore, newborn imitations are not stereotyped responses, at least not initially. Rather, they

[13] The foundational evidence for the face–emotion link has been undermined in several ways. Studies that have included both facial behavior and other putative measures of emotion have been scrutinized, re-analyzed, and meta-analyzed, and the overall results show little covariation or "coherence" between the two. Key experiments have been shown to have been misreported in ways that fail to support the basic emotion paradigm based on them. And, most important of all, new data demonstrate cultural diversity in facial displays while disproving the basic emotion assumption that humans pan-culturally "recognize" basic emotions from the predicted facial expressions. See Gendron et al. 2014; Crivelli et al. 2016a; 2016b; Duran et al. 2017; Fridlund 2017; Crivelli & Fridlund 2018; Barrett et al. 2019.

reported that it took time and effort for newborns to "correct" their behavior in order to produce a better fit with the adult model, even without any feedback from the adult. They therefore argued that "it seems more accurate to think of early imitation as intentional matching to the target provided by the other, rather than as a rigidly-organized reflexive response" (Meltzoff & Gopnik, 1993, 342; see also Meltzoff et al. 1991). Their claim contradicted the standard definition of imitation, which was generally reserved for the demonstration of the exact replication of both means and ends (Bard & Russell 1999, 91). Yet Meltzoff and Moore used the lack of precision in the initial imitation to argue that the baby's movements were not involuntary or reflex-like responses but deliberate, intentional actions. The apparent intentionality of the mimetic response helped the researchers to answer doubts about the existence of imitation in newborns by suggesting that imitations do occur but that investigators should not expect immediate, precise matches (Meltzoff & Moore 1983, 290; Butterworth 1999a, 72–73; Meltzoff 2002, 32–33). In addition, work on individual differences in neonatal responses helped explain the fragility and variability of the response (Heimann 1999).

It is worth asking what entitled Meltzoff and Moore to confidently apply the idea of self-correction to newborns on the basis of the response pattern they observed. What evidence was there for such a complex cognitive ability as recursive awareness in such tiny babies? Having the appearance of intentionality did not, in and of itself, establish that there was deliberate or intentional action, but this is what the authors claimed (for rejections of their interpretation in terms of response correction see, among others, Anisfeld 2005; Jones 2009; Ray & Heyes 2011; Vincini & Jhang 2018, 405–6).[14] It is also worth emphasizing that Meltzoff and Moore's proposal that the newborn was able to calibrate its facial movements in order to make a closer fit to the model's behavior amounted to the claim that what infants possess is a capacity for imitative trial-and-error learning. They not only asserted that neonates could imitate facial movements at birth, which was itself a very strong claim, they also made the even stronger suggestion that newborns could perceive the exact discrepancies between their own movements and that of the model and correct them through some kind of learning adjustment – a suggestion that bought Meltzoff and Moore some latitude in explaining the instability of the response.

In the course of long careers involving hundreds of publications, Meltzoff and Moore and other researchers developed several theories predicated on the reality of newborn imitation. It is these theories that Oostenbroek et al. 2016

[14] Bower had earlier claimed to demonstrate intentional reaching in newborns, based on their crying behavior, when their reaching for an object was frustrated because the object on display was only virtual (Bower et al. 1970a).

have suggested will have to be modified or discarded if neonatal imitation is disproved. In the following sections I will investigate the most important of them. Although the theories are closely intertwined, for the sake of clarity I have organized them into distinct topics, and will cover them in the following sections:

4.1 Neonatal Imitation and the Active Intermodal Mapping Hypothesis.
4.2 Mirror Neurons, Ideomotor, and Associationist Theories of Neonatal Imitation.
4.3 Neonatal Imitation and Theories of the Self.
4.4 Neonatal Imitation and the Nonconceptual Content of Perception.

4.1 Neonatal Imitation and the Active Intermodal Mapping Hypothesis

"The holy grail for cognitive and neuro-science theories of imitation is to elucidate the mechanism by which infants connect the felt but unseen movements of the self with the seen but unfelt movements of the other" (Meltzoff & Decety 2003, 491). Meltzoff and Moore here described the so-called *correspondence problem*. The problem posed is how sensory input generated by observing another's actions is converted into a recognizably similar or corresponding action on the part of the beholder, an enigma that has been described as "arguably the central scientific puzzle in imitation research" (Nehaniv & Dautenhahn 2002, 41; Brass & Heyes 2005). The purpose of Meltzoff and Moore's "Supramodal" or "Active Intermodal Mapping" hypothesis (hereafter AIM) was to offer a solution to that seemingly intractable problem.

At the start of their work on newborn imitation Meltzoff and Moore considered alternative interpretations of their findings. One was the theory that newborn imitation was based on a kind of Skinnerian learning with reinforcements administered by the experimenter, an explanation Meltzoff and Moore dismissed on the grounds that their procedures had eliminated that possibility. A second interpretation was that newborn imitations were fixed action patterns, triggered by innate releasing mechanisms, like those studied by the ethologists Konrad Lorenz and Nikko Tinbergen. This, too, was rejected because in Meltzoff and Moore's view the imitations they had observed were insufficiently stereotyped and appeared more deliberate and intentional. It also seemed to them that the fact that the infants imitated not one but four different facial gestures rendered this explanation "unwieldy" (Meltzoff & Moore 1977, 77).

In subsequent publications the authors also raised in order to discard what turned out to be one of the most enduring alternative explanation of their results: that the observed imitations were merely the result of the infant's arousal and hence were not true copies at all. Many different stimuli, researchers pointed out, could arouse the same kinds of movements described by Meltzoff and Moore, especially tongue protrusion. For example, Susan Jones showed that flashing colored lights, dangling toys, the sound of classical music, and other stimuli – none of which resembled a human modelling tongue protrusion– were also able to induce tongue protrusion in young infants. Might Meltzoff and Moore's results not be imitations, but reactions to a global state of arousal? (Jones, 1996; 2006). Meltzoff and Moore dismissed this arousal explanation on the grounds that, in the absence of controls of the kind involved in their "differential imitation" method, the findings could not be interpreted (Meltzoff & Moore 1977, 76; 1983, 277–79).

This left the explanation of infant imitation that Meltzoff and Moore favored, namely, that the movements they observed resulted from an innate matching process by which the newborn represents visually and proprioceptively perceived information "in a form common to both modalities." In other words, they argued that for neonatal imitation to occur there had to be a "common representational domain for perception and action" (Meltzoff & Prinz 2002, 8). In terms borrowed from Bower, in 1977 they proposed that: "The infant could thus compare the sensory information from his own unseen motor behavior to a 'supramodal' representation of the visually perceived gesture and construct the match required." And, in an accompanying note, they observed: "'Supramodal' is used, following T. Bower … to denote that the representation is not particular to one sensory modality alone." "In brief," they added:

> we hypothesize that the imitative responses observed are not innately organized and "released," but are accomplished through an active matching process and mediated by an abstract representational system. Our recent observations of facial imitation in six newborns – one only 60 minutes old – suggest to us that the ability to use intermodal equivalences is an innate ability of humans. If this is so, we must revise our current conceptions of infancy, which hold that such a capacity is the product of many months of postnatal development. The ability to act on the basis of abstract representations of a perceptually absent stimulus becomes the starting point for psychological development in infancy and not its culmination. (Meltzoff & Moore 1977, 78)

The authors repeated their claims in subsequent publications. In 1978 Moore and Meltzoff clarified the mapping process and declared it anti-Piagetian:

> The infant is thus envisaged as comparing his own (unseen) facial movements to what might be called a "supramodal representation" of the gestures he sees, and then as actively constructing the match required. Such a representation is termed "supramodal" (after Bower, 1974) inasmuch as it is not particular to

> one sensory modality … [T]his phenomenon raises serious questions about the Piagetian, action-based theory of infant sensorimotor development. The capacity for acting on the basis of an internal representation of the external world may not be the culmination of psychological development in infancy as Piaget conceived – but merely its starting-point. (Moore & Meltzoff 1978, 156–57)

Over time, the authors continued to use the term "supramodal," and also "intermodal," "transmodal," and "amodal," to describe the hypothetical AIM system. In 1979, Meltzoff and Borton claimed to have demonstrated tactile–visual intermodal perception in babies as young as 29 days, thereby further supporting their claims for the existence of a supramodal mapping system (Meltzoff & Borton 1979, 403–4). And in a 1982 paper on imitations performed after a gap of time, with reference to Molyneux's question of whether the unity of senses was innate or learned, and to the opinions of Bower and the Gibsons concerning the primordial unity of the senses, Meltzoff remarked:

> [W]e postulate that imitation, even this early imitation, involves active intermodal matching in which infants recognize an equivalence between the act seen and their own act which is done at a later time. That is our major claim about early imitation … Our corollary hypothesis is that this imitation is mediated by a representational system that unifies different modalities. Such a representational system does not register sense-specific elements, but rather utilizes what can be called "supramodal" or "transmodal" information. According to this view, information picked up by the proprioceptive and visual systems can be represented in a form common to both. This allows infants to compare information from their own unseen movements to a supramodal representation of the visually perceived model and to produce the motor match required. (Meltzoff 1982, 102)[15]

In other words, according to Meltzoff, the supramodal representations mediating imitation are neither sensory nor motor but "abstract" invariant representations forming a common code not tied to specific sensations (Meltzoff 1982, 108–9; see also Meltzoff & Moore 1995a, 87). In 1989 Meltzoff and Moore labeled their proposed supramodal system the "Active Intermodal Mapping" hypothesis or system (Meltzoff & Moore 1989, 961) (see Figure 2). This hypothesis has been the dominant explanatory model for neonatal imitation for the last 30 years. One issue the authors did not address or the AIM hypothesis explain, though, was what allows the infant to ignore movements that are not to be imitated. If the model posing a movement incidentally twitches her nose while protruding her tongue, will the infant

[15] See also Field et al. 1983; Fontaine 1984; Meltzoff & Moore, 1995a, 87; 1997; Bushnell 1998, 82–83

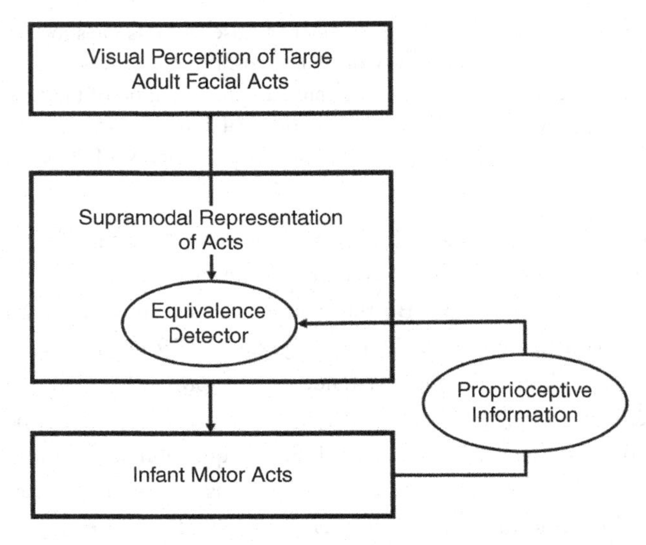

Figure 2. A Conceptual Schematic of the Active Intermodal Mapping Hypothesis (AIM). From Meltzoff, A. N. & Moore, M. K. (1997). Explaining Facial Imitation: A Theoretical Model. *Early Development and Parenting, 6, 180.* Reproduced by permission.

imitate that? It seems the newborn would have to solve the problem of the selectivity of the imitative response, or the problem of salience, a topic to which I will return.

As the passage quoted above makes clear, AIM is a representational system of perception. As such, it accords with the assumptions of the cognitive sciences and those of one of its best-known theorists, the philosopher Jerry Fodor (Fodor 1975; 1981). Thus, for Meltzoff and Moore the organism's cognitive relations to the world are mediated by a system of internal representations, a system whose processes they and Fodor have understood in computational terms. Meltzoff acknowledged the connection to Fodor's theorizing, whose influence was felt not only in the positing of internal representations mediating between the organism and the world but also in Fodor's conviction, following Chomsky, that the most fundamental operations of the mind are innate. Meltzoff eventually came to distinguish his views from Fodor's only in his description of his position as a "starting-state nativism" rather than Fodor's "final-state nativism." By this Meltzoff meant that Fodor believed that an infant's innate knowledge is at the level of adult commonsense psychology. But Meltzoff held that the newborn is provided with an innate foundation for building an adult psychology, surpassing Piaget's theorizing in this regard, but that at the start it does not possess full-blown adult knowledge. The baby has to develop it. However,

Meltzoff explained newborn capabilities, such as imitation, by appealing to the existence of internal representations along the lines of Fodor's claims (Meltzoff 2005, 74).

Although the general issue of representationalism in the cognitive sciences lies outside the scope of my analysis, it must be emphasized that cogent objections, especially as those assumptions had been systematized by Fodor, have been put forward for some time (Coulter 1982; 1985; 2008; Williams 1999; Coulter & Sharrock 2007). Nevertheless – and in spite of Fodor's subsequent retreat from some of his more extreme views – it is rare for psychologists to appreciate the strength of objections to conceiving the mind in internal computational-representationalist terms. Meltzoff and Moore are no exceptions in this regard. They did more than posit an innate representational system capable of performing perceptual-motor matching at birth. As I've observed, they considered the imitative matches to be intentional actions, as evidenced by the claim that the newborn appeared able to correct its movements in response to the model in order to make its imitative matches more exact. It was the apparent absence of any sign of automaticity in the workings of neonatal imitation that lent plausibility to Meltzoff and Moore's suggestion that the infant is capable of the mental-cognitive act of "recognizing" the similarity of the model to itself – what they labeled the "like me" experience. One of the issues that remained unclear, however, was at what level this act of "recognition" was supposed to operate, whether at the phenomenological level of conscious personal experience or at the level of subpersonal computational processes – or both.

But how exactly was the AIM system itself supposed to work? One can sympathize with Susan Jones, a long-time critic of neonatal imitation claims, when she observed that the AIM model could not credibly explain any purported imitations because it remained sparse, abstract, and untested (Jones 2005, vol. 1, 208; see also Jones 2016). Researcher Cecilia Heyes likewise noted the underspecification inherent in the AIM postulate, making it "difficult to test without clear hypotheses about the 'common currency,' about the nature of the nonsensory 'amodal' properties used for comparison and the processes through which they are derived from sensory input" (Heyes 2005, 167). And in 2018 Vincini and Jhang commented not only on the equivocal nature of the empirical findings on neonatal imitation but also on the "lack of clarity at the level of explanations" (Vincini & Jhang 2018, 396).

Indeed, there is a sense in which the AIM hypothesis simply appeared to restate in seemingly scientific or information-processing language the very correspondence problem of imitative matching that it was attempting to solve. In this regard, it's as if all the crucial terms of the AIM hypothesis functioned merely as placeholders. To the question "How does the newborn match its movements to those of an adult?" the answer appeared to be "Because there is a supramodal representational system that can perform the match." This is particularly evident in the function assigned to the "Equivalence Detector" in Meltzoff and Moore's depiction of the flow of information in AIM (see Figure 2). How was the "Equivalence Detector" supposed to work? Without further clarification, the infant's ability to detect the equivalence between its movements and those of a model remained unexplained.

AIM also contained an apparent incoherence concerning precisely the mechanism proposed. According to Meltzoff and Moore's formulation, and following the Gibsons and Bower, the visual and proprioceptive systems functioning together in the AIM system shared a unified, abstract perceptual code. As Meltzoff and Moore typically described the process:

> The fact that young infants can imitate facial gestures shows that the perception and production of human acts are intrinsically intertwined. We hypothesized that infants can represent human movement patterns they see and ones they perform using the same mental code ... There is thus something like an act space or primitive body scheme that allows the infant to unify the visual and motor/proprioceptive information into one common "supramodal" framework. This supramodal act space is not restricted to modality-specific information (visual, tactile, motor, etc.). (Meltzoff 2007a, 130)

The emphasis fell on the unity or identity of the visual and proprioceptive "mental codes" held to subserve imitative matching. The same emphasis on the similarity of such codes informed Prinz and Meltzoff's 2002 rejection of the language of "translation" to describe the matching process, precisely because the authors did not think any "translation" between codes was involved. According to them, translation suggested the existence of an incommensurability between the visual and motor codes, with each code belonging to its own representational domain, which would then need to be linked together by some mechanism or system. Prinz and Meltzoff, by contrast, defended what they called a similarity-based or "equivalence" system, according to which there exist common codes in the representations of the infant's perceptions and its own performances, allowing the newborn to detect or recognize the equivalence between the facial movements they see and those they feel, and hence to perform imitations at birth. The authors therefore characterized the AIM hypothesis as offering a way to "overcome the limitations of the classical Cartesian view of separate and incommensurate systems" by proposing a role for "similarity-based" matching. As they observed: "Within the common representational domain, perception and action can talk to each other directly in the same representational language, and there is no need for translation anymore.

One can induce the other by virtue of similarity." They described the AIM mechanism as embodying this basic "logic of similarity" (Prinz & Meltzoff 2002, 8). Research by Jean Decety on common perception and action coding in the brain as demonstrated by research using functional imaging (research on which Meltzoff sometimes appeared as a coauthor) likewise appeared to support the idea of similarity-based imitation mechanisms (Meltzoff & Decety 2003).

But a problem arose. If, according to the AIM model, the infant and adult in an imitative scenario shared the same abstract representational codes, how was the infant supposed to grasp the differences between its movements and those of the adult, differences on which the baby's capacity for the intentional correction of its matching movements was held to depend? Some process or mechanism allowing the infant to compare those differences had to exist, differences that the hypothesized mapping system founded on the alleged unity of the senses appeared to be unable to provide. In short, there seemed to be a fundamental incoherence at the center of the AIM hypothesis.

By 1995 Meltzoff and Moore had begun to confront this issue by proposing that there had to be some differentiation in the hypothesized supramodal system of representations to prevent confusion between the imitator and the imitated, or between copy and model. Thus, on the one hand, the authors still maintained that imitation relied on a system of unified visual and motor-proprioceptive codes. On the other hand, they now granted that the same system possessed the ability to distinguish between the infant's and the model's representations in the imitation scenario.

The representational system had to contain the possibility of differentiation for several reasons. First, the system did not automatically convert perceptions into actions: babies were said to be able to improve and defer their imitative responses, suggesting the existence of intermediary representations and not simply a mechanical transduction. Second, the fact that the newborn appeared capable of adjusting its imitative matches suggested that information about its movements had to be available for comparison with the adult's actions, without the visual representations of the adult's behavior becoming confused with baby's own multiple motor attempts. Third, infants showed a special interest in being copied themselves, and appeared to have the capacity to recognize when this occurred. That recognition likewise implied a distinction between the representation of their own bodies and those of others.

On the basis of these considerations, Meltzoff and Moore now proposed that the representational codes subserving imitation were both similar *and* different, unified *and* differentiated – although they did not specify how and when the representations were differentiated or re-unified. In their words:

> Although both representations use the supramodal language, they are not confused. The cognitive act is to compare these two representations, in one case to match one's own acts with the other's (imitative correction) and in the other case to detect being matched oneself (recognizing being imitated). Thus the mental code may use a supramodal "language," but the mind is not one undifferentiated supramodal whole. (Meltzoff & Moore, 1995b, 53)

So far as I have been able to determine, at only one point did Meltzoff and Moore explicitly acknowledge the problem they were facing. In a 1997 article that Meltzoff has frequently cited as containing one of his and Moore's most important theoretical statements concerning the AIM mechanism, the two authors admitted that at first sight the "thoroughly amodal perceptual system" risked recreating the very lack of differentiation between the newborn self and that of the adult as posited by James, Freud, and Piaget. In the past Meltzoff and Moore had decried the idea of such an original "adualism." But they now conceded the dilemma:

> Imitation requires some cross-modal metric of equivalence. This raises a new problem. If infants can perceive self and other in equivalent terms, can they be told apart? Is there any perceptual distinction between self and other for the young baby? Piaget and Freud wrote elegantly of the initial "confusion," "adualism," and lack of distinction between self and other. In more modern terms, if one invokes a thoroughly amodal perceptual system to mediate imitation, this (ironically) recreates a Piagetian lack of differentiation.

Rather than resolving this conceptual dilemma, Meltzoff and Moore appealed instead to the ostensible empirical evidence:

> A little data goes a long way in sorting this out. As we have seen, imitative acts can be corrected to achieve a more veridical match. Thus information about the infant's acts is available for comparison to a representation of the adult's act. More importantly for the problem at hand, representation of the target derived from the external world is not confused with or modified by the infants' own motor attempts. This suggests a differentiation such that representation of the other's body is separate from representation of the infant's body. Although both representations use the supramodal "language" of organ relations, self and other are not just one undifferentiated whole. (Meltzoff & Moore 1997, 188)[16]

Thus, Meltzoff and Moore appealed to evidence of the infant's supposed ability to correct its imitative matches in order to rescue the supramodal hypothesis from its central incoherence.

[16] Meltzoff and Moore suggested that the identification or individuation of the corresponding body parts or organs in the baby was a first step in generating the imitative response. They also emphasized the role of "body babbling" – repetitive movements of the infant's limbs and facial muscles, starting in the womb– in mapping the links between body parts and the relations between organs (Meltzoff & Moore 1997, 183–84).

Of course, on a theoretical level this explanation was no solution at all. It simply muddied the waters, especially because it contradicted everything the authors had previously claimed about the original unity of the abstract codes involved in the supramodal perceptual-action system. In short, if in the original conception of the AIM hypothesis the imitative link between perception and action was held to be a function of commensurate or similarity-based representations, in the revised conception of the AIM hypothesis the link was held to be a function of incommensurate or difference-based representations. Or perhaps it would be more accurate to say that Meltzoff and Moore now presented the AIM system as a mechanism that somehow combined both differentiated and undifferentiated or unified, "supramodal" coding elements.

To confuse matters further, after 1997 Meltzoff and his colleagues continued to represent AIM as fundamentally a similarity-based system (e.g., Meltzoff 2002, 25; Prinz & Meltzoff 2002, 9). Not all agree. In 2017, at the height of the renewed debate over neonatal imitation, Vincini, Jhang, Buder, and Gallagher critically assessed the AIM hypothesis by focusing on the model's inclusion of differences between perception and action representations. Describing Meltzoff and Moore's claims in their 1997 paper, the authors remarked:

> Imitation is achieved through a "comparison" computation described in Meltzoff and Moore (1997, pp. 185–186). The comparison has two inputs: one is visually perceived action features and the other is proprioceptively experienced action features. Specifically, the computation compares the "configural relations between organs" and/or the "speed, duration, and manner" of the modeled action with the configural organ relations and/or dynamic properties of the infant's own actions … If the two inputs are dissimilar, the output is a "mismatch," and then the infant executes a new attempt. If the two inputs are similar, the output is a "match" and the infant has recognized the similarity between her own and the other's actions. For this reason, imitation entails the recognition experience or the basic perception: "That seen event is like this felt event" or "Here is something like me" … Note that it is essential to AIM that the two inputs entering the computation are clearly separate, as shown in Meltzoff and Moore's … schematic of AIM. If there are not two distinct inputs, the idea of a comparison for the detection of the similarities and dissimilarities falls apart. Hence, Meltzoff and Moore (1997) insist that the visual representations of the modeled actions must be "independent" or "separate" from the corresponding proprioceptive representations. (Vincini et al. 2017a, 6; see also Vincini & Jhang 2018, 403)[17]

[17] I note that Vincini and colleagues labeled AIM the "Active Intermodal Matching" hypothesis, rather than the "Active Intermodal Mapping" hypothesis (Vincini et al. 2017a; Vincini & Jhang 2018).

This was a fair description of the AIM hypothesis as described by Meltzoff and Moore in 1997, since it drew attention to the fact that imitative matching depended as much on the perception of the difference between the codes connecting self to other as on the perception of similarities. No matter if Vincini et al. ignored the long history of speculation, going back in the modern period at least as far as the Gibsons and Bower, about the original unity of the senses to which Meltzoff and Moore had appealed when they first announced their AIM hypothesis. What Vincini et al.'s discussion helped foreground was the shift that had occurred in Meltzoff and Moore's description of the AIM mechanism when in their 1997 paper they acknowledged the importance of the incommensurability between the codes governing newborn imitation. Vincini and Jhang therefore suggested that, for Meltzoff and Moore, the role of AIM's "supramodal" mechanism, defined as a separately evolved system, was now precisely to "overcome the fundamental incommensurability" between perception and action by being sensitive to information derived from both sources (Vincini & Jhang 2018, 403–5).

Nevertheless, it is unclear how, by reformulating their AIM hypothesis in this way, Meltzoff and Moore could have hoped to solve the all-important correspondence problem. Suggesting that there are such differentiated codes, and that the infant is able thereby to compare them, simply redescribes the problem but does nothing to explain it. What tells the infant that the facial movements they see an adult perform do or do not correspond to its own? To accomplish this, it seems the infant would already need to have resolved the correspondence problem in the first place.

The situation is not improved but merely postponed by appealing on cognitive science grounds, as Meltzoff and Moore also did, to a putative internal computational program that does the work of "recognition." This move assumes that such a computational program can mimic or replicate the interpretations and appropriate forms of human responses that are involved in the many different kinds of recognition that exist. But this is precisely the problem that needs to be solved (see in this connection Coulter 1987). We still have no idea how the computational program abstracts from the environment the relevant visual "information" and links it to the relevant proprioceptive input to achieve the intentional imitative match. We especially do not know how the program handles the puzzle of salience, which is to say, how it recognizes what are to count as the relevant stimulus features to be extracted from the environment, or how it matches those features to the relevant proprioceptive codes in any of the specific contexts in which such performances take place. In short, as the philosopher Shaun Gallagher put it, the AIM hypothesis offered "a set of theoretical black boxes representing 'comparison function,' 'act equivalence,' 'recognition of my own capability, etc.,'" but without explaining how those boxes might be filled (Gallagher 2001, 98).

4.2 Mirror Neurons, Ideomotor, and Associationist Theories of Neonatal Imitation

Does appealing to mirror neurons help fill those black boxes? When mirror neurons were first identified in the 1990s it was not a difficult step to conclude that they might be the vehicle for the imitative matching process. The discovery in macaque monkeys of neurons that fire both when the animal performs an action and when it only observes a similar action performed by another seemed to have an obvious application to the phenomenon of imitation, including newborn imitation. As the well-known cognitive neuroscientist Greg Hickok remarked: "Mirror neurons seem tailor-made to assume the role of the neural mechanism for imitation" (Hickok 2014, 188).

Gallagher was one of the first scholars to argue that mirror neurons could provide the neonatal imitative mechanism that the AIM hypothesis was seen by him to lack. "I propose," he wrote, "that in part this model can be filled in on the neurological level by the functioning of mirror neurons … Mirror neurons thus constitute an intermodal link between the visual perception of action or dynamic expression, and the *intrasubjective, proprioceptive* sense of one's own capabilities" (Gallagher 2001, 98–99; his emphasis). Many others made similar claims (see, for example, Iacobini 2009). Gallagher would later change his views when, in the 2017 paper with Vincini and others already mentioned, he rejected the mirror neuron approach to imitation in favor of a similarity-based associationist model (Vincini et al. 2017a; and see below).

However, Meltzoff and Moore recognized that mirror neuron explanations of imitation were not an easy fit with their work. This is because according to them, infants intentionally make the close match that defines a genuine imitation, whereas mirror neurons were held to function automatically, unless inhibited in some way. Neurological solutions in the form of automatic mirror neuron resonances were therefore difficult to reconcile with the claimed intentional nature of neonatal imitation. For Meltzoff and his colleagues, then, the basic mirror neuron machinery might well play an important role in neonatal imitation, but "something more" than direct resonance had to be involved. This was the message of Meltzoff and Decety in a paper of 2003: "Humans do not simply directly resonate … Intending to imitate already tunes regions beyond simple motor resonance … [F]eatures of human imitation may go beyond the workings of the mirror neurons *per se* … Something more is needed to prompt and support behavioral imitation" (Meltzoff & Decety 2003, 493–94). In other words, mirror neuron explanations appeared to bypass the kinds of cognitive-intentional abilities that, according to Meltzoff and Moore, shape the imitative reactions of newborn imitation (Marshall & Meltzoff 2014; see also Brass & Heyes 2005; Meltzoff 2007a, 130–34; Vincini et al. 2017b, 5).

Meltzoff and Moore's position has something in common with that of Hickok, whose recent critique of mirror neuron research emphasizes the selective nature of imitation (Hickok 2014). Hickok has therefore cast doubt on approaches that invoke these neurons to explain the perception-action link. As Hickok is well aware, many researchers have theorized imitation as an automatic process for which mirror neurons would seem the obvious mediators. Thus, in 1999, in a well-known paper, social psychologists Tanya Chartrand and John Bargh coined the term "The Chameleon Effect" to describe the ways in which adult humans apparently automatically, unconsciously, and unintentionally mimic the movements, facial expressions, and behaviors of others. In their joint research, Chartrand and Bargh have focused on postural mimicry, which is to say, on the movements performed when people inadvertently imitate or copy the behavior of others by adopting the others' bodily actions (Chartrand & Bargh 1999). But these authors have extended their analyses to include all kinds of imitation, including facial mimicry in newborns, the so-called emotional contagion observed when people copy the facial expressions of others, the contagion of yawning, the imitative effects of unconscious priming, and many other phenomena.

Throughout their discussions of what they have called the "automaticity of being," Chartrand and Bargh have emphasized the idea that the Chameleon Effect is the result of an imitative process that occurs blindly, as it were, because it happens unconsciously and without intention or purpose (Bargh & Chartrand 1999).[18] It is therefore not surprising that they have been interested in mirror neurons, since these neurons would appear to offer precisely the kind of neurological mechanism required to explain such imitative effects. Thus, Chartrand and Bargh have referred to mirror neuron research in order to claim that perceiving someone else engaging in a behavior is neurologically similar to performing that behavior oneself (Chartrand et al. 2005, 334; see also Bargh 2011, 631–32). Moreover, Vittorio Gallese, one of the codiscoverers of mirror neurons, has cited the Chameleon Effect as a phenomenon that can be explained by the operation of these cells (Gallese 2007, 94).

[18] As is by now well known, in 2012 a controversy erupted over the replicability of one of Bargh's most famous experimental studies of the priming effect of words associated with old age on the walking speeds of experimental subjects. But a discussion of that controversy lies outside the scope of my analysis.

But such views have left a question that has come to haunt the entire literature on the question of the automaticity of imitation: Why does imitation have its limits? Why is it that we do not mimic every behavior or movement or facial expression that we encounter but instead confine or adapt our mimicries according to the setting or context or social circumstances? If the process of imitation is a hardwired, involuntary response mediated by mirror neurons, how can it also be highly selective? Even the theorists of the Chameleon Effect have been obliged to recognize the fact of selectivity (Chartrand et al. 2005, 343). In fact, as Chartrand, Bargh, and other contagion and mirror neuron theorists have acknowledged, we would soon go insane if we were to spend our days resonating nonselectively, immoderately, and automatically to whatever facial or other signals we encounter.[19]

I think it is fair to say that imitation theorists have been scrambling in recent years to account for this obvious fact. Their response has been to admit the social aspect of imitation while also to defend the idea of the automaticity of the imitative process – not an easy trick to pull off (Van Baaren et al. 2009). The problem of the selectivity of imitation is at the center of Hickok's book *The Myth of Mirror Neurons*, published in 2014 – to my mind, the most convincing analysis and critique of mirror neuron theory to appear so far (see also Jones 2016). Hickok accuses mirror neuron theorists – and by extension, theorists of imitation and contagion, including theorists of newborn imitation – of forgetting that imitation and mirror neuron activity are subordinate to cognitive goals and purposes. He emphasizes that although it is sometimes important for animals to copy conspecifics, at other times it is imperative for them to select completely different, "anti-mirror" or "logical relation" movements, such as blocking or fleeing from an attack, or submitting to a grooming gesture. Mimicry is therefore highly selective. "Even mirror neurons are smart in this respect," Hickok observes. "They don't resonate willy-nilly with any old action; they only resonate with actions that have a purpose, defined not by the movements themselves but by the movements in a particular context, by some deeper understanding." He therefore suggests that "something more is needed to explain why some gestures are mimicked and others are not." He remarks:

> [U]nconscious mimicry serves a social function … Some bit of social machinery is at the core of the process, not the mimicry itself. It's not that we are social because we mimic; we mimic because we are social. This is not just an alternative framing of the relation. The two perspectives have different explanatory power. If we try to use unconscious mimicry as an innate

[19] For a detailed discussion and critique of one well-known experiment by Wicker et al. 2003, purporting to demonstrate the role of mirror neurons in the empathic transmission of the emotion of disgust, see Leys 2012.

> foundation on which sociability naturally grows, we have no explanation for why we don't mimic everyone all the time. How can unconscious, "automatic" mimicry be so selective? If, however, unconscious mimicry is a consequence of a social brain, then social states … can serve as the "something more" that guides imitation. (Hickok 2014, 204)

Indeed, as Hickok observes, several experiments by Catmur, Heyes and others have demonstrated that the mirror neuron system is not hardwired. Rather, it is a highly malleable, plastic, sensorimotor system that is so pliable, so open to diverse learning situations during individual development, that it is capable of producing a wide variety of responses, including both "congruent" or "mirror" movements and "non-congruent" or "anti-mirror" actions. These findings have led Catmur, Heyes and others to propose that, rather than viewing the coupling between perception and movement as innate and fixed, it is instead the result of associative learning during sensorimotor development (Catmur et al. 2007; Heyes 2005; Hickok 2014, 53–58, 195–96).[20]

On the basis of these and related considerations, Hickok is even able to explain the inconvenient fact, namely, that macaque monkeys, in which mirror neurons were first discovered, do not imitate, or at least do not do it very well. They are capable of social learning but they cannot perform the kinds of imitation that are routine in humans (for a brief summary of the evidence see Jones 2016). The reason, Hickok proposes, is that having mirror neurons is not sufficient for mimicry to take place, because mimicry is a social skill that depends on the presence of higher-order cognitive abilities that are distinctly human. That is why, as Hickok also observes, human chameleons do not imitate everyone all the time. Indeed, he points out that excessive and inappropriate imitations, such as those seen in echolalia, or the automatic repetition of vocalizations, are symptomatic of certain neurological disorders (Hickok 2014, 203).

Moreover, Hickok notes that Meltzoff and Moore's claims for the existence of imitation in newborns, implying an innate tendency to mimic at birth, have not gone unchallenged. He cites Susan Jones' critical assessment of the experiments and her view that claims for newborn imitation lack supporting evidence. Instead, existing data suggests that infants do not imitate until their second year and that imitation of different kinds of behavior emerges at different ages. Jones therefore concludes: "The evidence is consistent with a dynamic systems account in which the ability to imitate is not an inherited, specialized module,

[20] It remains an open question, however, whether the human mirror system operates as "dumbly" or as independently of cognitive mechanisms as Heyes's Associative Sequence Learning theory suggests (see Gallese et al. 2011 for discussions).

but is instead the emergent product of a system of social, cognitive, and motor components, each with its own developmental history" (Jones 2009, 2325).

Thus, the mirror neuron mechanism itself may well be primitive but, Hickok argues, what matters is knowing what and when to imitate. Macaque brains have the mirror neuron machinery but lack the necessary cognitive accompaniments to make intelligent use of it, which is why, unlike humans, they are unable to take full advantage of imitation for language learning and social networking. The human brain, on the other hand, is built to use imitation if and when it is beneficial. Hickok therefore concludes that we humans may well have the same type of mirror neurons as macaque monkeys, "but we differ in the cognitive (information-processing) mechanisms that have evolved to put those fundamentally associative mechanisms to good use. And that is why humans ape better than apes ape" (Hickok 2014, 206). Meltzoff and Decety made a similar point when in 2003 they observed that the mimetic skills of newborns seemed to be beyond the capabilities of mirror neurons (Meltzoff & Decety 2003, 493–94).

In sum, for both Hickok and Meltzoff and Decety, "something more" than mirror neurons is required to explain why some behaviors are mimicked and not others. For Meltzoff and Moore that "something more" involves the role of intentions, while for Hickok it involves "social states": for these authors, it is those intentions or social states that guide the selection of imitations. (How these authors theorize the nature of intentionality or social states, or indeed whether they can adequately do so within the terms of the cognitive science approach they adopt, is another story, and one that I cannot address here; see Leys 2017). Of course, Meltzoff and Moore's arguments are premised on the idea that an innate capacity for imitation at birth is a proven empirical fact. But if it turns out that Oostenbroek et al.'s criticisms of the empirical data are valid, then the need to explain neonatal imitation will disappear. This still leaves a great deal to understand about the acquisition and development of the infant's cognitive-intentional abilities and indeed its imitative skills (for a recent summary of findings, see Jones 2016), but those abilities and skills can be studied developmentally and not as derivatives of neonatal imitation.

Do any other theories designed to explain neonatal imitation offer alternative ways forward? In several recent publications, Vincini and colleagues reject the idea that mirror neuron theory can explain neonatal imitation, but they do so for very different reasons than those offered by Meltzoff and Moore (or indeed than those offered by Hickok, whose work they do not mention). Vincini and his coauthors deny that there is an innate propensity in infants to imitate at birth. They argue that *if*, nevertheless, under certain conditions some neonates do appear to imitate certain movements – and the authors treat this as an open question– it is because, as a result of learned associations, their actions have been passively induced to match movements presented by the model, as long as stronger motivations do not intervene. The imitative response, they write, is

> "induced" or "suggested" by the presentation of the model. The modeled act evokes a motor habit that can be implemented. *The mere evocation of an action possibility is a motivation, or "enticer," to fulfill it*, when stronger motivations are not conditioning the newborn otherwise. In other words, once an action possibility has been awakened, this being-awakened makes that action more prominent in the range of action possibilities that constitute the background; thus, *other things being equal* (i.e. if stronger, unpredictable impulses do not favor other responses over the imitative response), the infant will be more likely to enact the action possibility that has come to stand out.
>
> No costly comparison, no recognition, no specialized module, no intermediary step of identification, no intention to match or test other people's identity, just a basic process of association and the resulting solicitation. (Vincini & Jhang 2018, 415; their emphases)

This is a perception–action model of imitation, with roots in Wolfgang Prinz's recent and William James's earlier ideomotor formulations, according to which the baby's spontaneous movements, such as its movements of the tongue, under the right conditions can be passively elicited to move in the same way as a model, because of the similarity in the internal computational representations of the baby's movements and the visual representations of the model's actions. On this scenario, the basis for the match is the baby's own spontaneous movements. The more frequent the baby's spontaneous movements, the easier it should be to induce those movements mimetically by the model's similar movements – as demonstrated by the fact that tongue protrusions and mouth openings, which the neonate performs naturally, are the most frequently observed imitations.

Vincini et al. call their theory the "Association by Similarity Theory" (hereafter AST), thereby indicating that it is an associationist learning theory. According to them, imitation is a performance that is induced after birth by the associations made between the spontaneous actions the baby performs and the posed facial movements of the model. The infant does not intend to make a match or deliberately copy the adult's movements; it is passively induced to do so because of the similarity between shared representational codes. The authors claim that their Association by Similarity Theory is preferable to Meltzoff and Moore's Active Intermodal Mapping hypothesis because it is more parsimonious – especially because it assumes less than the AIM model does about the newborn's cognitive abilities. According to Vincini et al., neither intention nor cognition are involved in neonatal imitation. The phenomenon therefore has none of the implications for social cognition that Meltzoff and Moore have attributed to it, such as its role in the infant's experience of selfhood, the development of a theory of mind, empathy and other social skills. "[I]nfants do not actively intend to match the behavior of others but, rather, tend to respond in a way that is more passively elicited," the authors state (Vincini et al. 2017b, 38).

Moreover, Vincini et al. argue that AST accounts better for the empirical evidence than does Meltzoff and Moore's AIM hypothesis. For instance, since according to AST there is no intention to imitate, slight differences in the baby's affective state can influence the outcome, thereby explaining why the experimental findings are so variable. If the experimental results are the outcome of a complex interplay between the infant's repertoire of spontaneous movements, its affective state, and an adult's movements – variables that are hard to control experimentally – no wonder the research findings are not very robust. Indeed, AST is compatible with the idea that differential imitation in newborns may only be detectable in extremely controlled experimental conditions and is "practically not detectable in natural settings" (Vincini & Jhang 2018, 417). Vincini et al. thus suggest that the phenomenon of neonatal imitation may be an artifact of the experiments themselves. This idea has led the AST authors to make various methodological recommendations for how best to carry out experiments in order to test AST as an explanation of neonatal imitation.

There is something undeniably attractive about Vincini et al.'s proposals. The authors offer an explanation for decades of dispute about the existence of newborn imitation, while leaving open the possibility that the results of experiments which have appeared to demonstrate such imitations are not completely discredited, but may merely have been the outcome of the proposed associative mechanism. Moreover, the authors downplay arguably hyperbolic claims by Meltzoff and Moore concerning the newborn's cognitive abilities by treating any signs of neonatal imitation as merely the outcome of such associative mechanisms, not of an innate, special-purpose cognitive mechanism that has evolved for that purpose. Following suggestions by Ray and Heyes (Ray & Heyes 2011), Vincini et al. reinterpret the infant's apparent "correction" of an initial lack of a match between its movements and model – a correction that Meltzoff and Moore have long attributed to the infant's intentional efforts to make a better fit – as merely the result of an "increase in vigor [and amplitude] with response repetition, or … perceptual learning … the formation of a better perceptual representation of the modeled movement with repeated exposures" (Vincini et al. 2017a, 6). Vincini et al.'s proposals are also potentially appealing because they suggest ways in which their associationist explanation of newborn imitation might be put to stringent experimental tests by specifying certain methodological requirements.

However, questions and concerns remain. With reference to Vincini et al.'s specific laboratory recommendations, in a recent paper Davis et al., in a meta-analysis of the neonatal imitation findings, have concluded that: "On the whole, the argument that specific differences in methodology are critical to the effect … is not supported by the current data" (Davis et al, 2020, quoted by permission). It remains to be seen how Vincini et al. will respond to that conclusion. But it is also difficult to understand how AST could explain the putative phenomenon of neonatal imitation. What is crucial to AST, in contrast to Meltzoff and Moore's AIM hypothesis as essentially understood by Vincini et al., and also in contrast to mirror neuron theory, is that the AST mechanism is a "common coding" or similarity-based theory. As we have seen, Vincini et al. have criticized Meltzoff and Moore's 1997 statement of their AIM hypothesis on the grounds that it requires an incommensurability between the visual and proprioceptive codes involved in imitation in order for the baby to recognize whether a match has been made. They also fault mirror neuron accounts of neonatal imitation for similarly assuming a differentiation between sensory and motor codes. Mirror neuron theories, they argue, have the virtue of downplaying the role of cognition in neonatal imitation, so central to Meltzoff and Moore's approach, but they are flawed as explanations of neonatal mimicry because they, too, depend on the idea of separate visual and motor representations.

However, for AST *all* that is required to explain neonatal imitation is the similarity between the infant's and adult's representational codes. As the authors state:

> AST hypothesizes that, when the infant sees the modeled action, the representational resources used in vision to represent the morphokinetic features of the action are the same resources that have been used to represent those morphokinetic features in proprioception. In other words, AST postulates a representational overlap. In this way, AST posits that the visual representation of an action involves representational resources that have been wired up with the motor components of a global action representation in spontaneous execution. Because of this prior association, the activation of the overlap area in visual processing will tend to activate the other areas with which it was habitually linked in action processing. In this way, a habitual action possibility is reawakened, and, if the infant does not have stronger impulses that lead it to behave otherwise, it will adhere to this action possibility, i.e. it will execute the act that we designate as "imitative." There is no comparison and no recognition that "That seen event is like this felt event." There is simply first a perception and then an impulse to act in a certain way; association by similarity regulates which perception activates which action tendency. (Vincini & Jhang 2018, 412)

Vincini et al. even criticize Wolfgang Prinz, from whose ideomotor theory the AST mechanism is derived, because the latter has recently expanded his views in order to accommodate other perception–action theories, such as that of Catmur and Heyes, based on the contiguity between perceptual and motor representations, rather than on their similarity. Vincini et al. reject Prinz's latest views as a "hybrid" approach that fails to recognize that similarity is the only mechanism at work in newborn imitation (Vincini et al., 2017a, 8–9, note 10; see also Prinz 2012, 66–68).

But how is Vincini et al.'s similarity-based model supposed to work? The authors cite some of the literature on the philosophical problems long connected with claims for the role of similarity-based explanations in psychology and the cognitive sciences. Although they do not pursue the issue, they appear to believe that those problems have been overcome. Yet it is not obvious that this is the case. Indeed, arguing that the AST mechanism operates according to the principle of "the 'functional role' of similarity" risks begging the question. The authors comment:

> [F]or both phenomenological and Hebbian models of perception, association by similarity is not the recognition of a particular relationship between objects. Rather, it is merely the process that regulates the activation of meanings that constitute the content of perception. In other words, in order to perceive a stimulus as an object of a particular kind, one does not have to compare (an indefinite number of) objects; instead, it suffices to activate the complex representation that is most strongly associated with the features presented by the stimulus. (Vincini & Jhang 2018, 410)

But given the acknowledged fact that similarity-based judgments or decisions are context-dependent, how does the similarity-based associative mechanism proposed by Vincini et al. identify which of all the possibilities are the relevant features presented by the stimulus for the match? The question is whether such a similarity-based system can cope with the view, as expressed by Nelson Goodman in a celebrated article, that "Circumstances alter similarities" (Goodman 1972, 445). It is unclear whether the solution proposed by Vincini et al. is as impervious to Goodman's critique of similarity as they appear to believe. For example, in response to concerns about the importance of context, Tversky's well-known feature-based approach to similarity had to be revised by replacing a context-insensitive similarity scale with "a *set* of scales ... containing a scale *sC* for each context *C*" (Decock & Douven 2011, 66). But how would one develop a scale for each context? One would need another context to determine the first context, and so on ad infinitum. The risk in similarity-based approaches to perception and action is thus one of infinite regress. In short, if imitation is a matter of context all the way down, AST does not explain how imitative matches occur. Instead, like the AIM hypothesis to which it is opposed, it seems that, by regarding similarities as self-evident, it presumes the very matching or correspondence process it is meant to solve.[21]

To repeat: the challenge faced by associationist theories of the kind embraced by Vincini et al. – and this applies as well to the similarity-based or supramodal hypothesis as first proposed by Meltzoff and Moore – is to explain why, among the many properties presented to the infant by an adult's movements, only certain ones are selected as the relevant ones for a similarity-based explanation. What counts as the "same" or "similar" properties or codes in the various situations a baby finds itself at the start of life, such that the posited association mechanism induces a match? This is the problem Hickok has addressed by highlighting the necessary role of cognition in selecting the relevant imitative responses according to the goals, intentions, and purposes of the organism.

The difficulty is that of specifying which properties become associated when multiple properties are co-instantiated. "Some would argue that this problem is a symptom of a larger issue: trying to use extensional criteria to specify intentional content," Eric Mandelbaum has observed in an overview of associationist theories in psychology; "Associationists need a criterion for which of the coextensive properties will in fact be learned, and which not" (Mandelbaum 2015, n.p.). The trouble is that there are multiple attributes by which any number of stimuli could be perceived as "similar" at any one moment. Which attribute will the infant use? Take, for example, the Wisconsin Card Sorting Test. The cards differ by the number of symbols, the types of symbol, and the colors of the symbols they display. The examiner lays out one card of each type in a different pile, and then gives the examinee the rest of the cards one by one, asking him or her to put each card in the "correct" pile. The trick is that only the examiner knows the rules. So if the test subject is given a card with three red diamonds, should she put the card in the pile with red symbols, with diamond shapes, or the three symbols? Only by the examiner's "right" or "wrong" feedback is the subject able to guess the rule, and it takes multiple trials to abstract it (Berg 1948). This is a test of frontal lobe function – that is, of cognitive skills. It is this test that ideomotor theorists believe occurs "naturally" and automatically: they believe that amid all the combinatorial possibilities, the newborn baby somehow knows how which are the relevant domains and thus

[21] For a further elaboration of his perception–action or "direct perception" view that early infant development can be explained by the similarity between "percepts" alone, see Vincini 2020. In this paper, the author appears to abandon his previously agnostic position on the reality of newborn imitation by endorsing the view that imitation does not take off before 9–10 months (Vincini 2020, 180). But the question of whether the terms of Vincini's 2020 analysis are adequate to explain the general phenomena of infant development will have to be addressed elsewhere.

solves the correspondence problem based only on the perceived similarity between representations. But is this plausible?

In this regard, Vincini et al.'s associationist proposal about the cause of neonatal imitation appears to face just as many challenges as does Meltzoff and Moore's AIM hypothesis: both appear to fall short of being able to explain the correspondence problem central to neonatal imitation, to whatever extent it may occur.

4.3 Neonatal Imitation and Theories of the Self

In this section I examine the widely held claim that the newborn possesses a primitive, interpersonal sense of self.

One of the major ideas founded on the concept of neonatal imitation has been Meltzoff and Meltzoff's assertion that newborns possess a primordial awareness of the self, enabling them to differentiate themselves from other human beings. The authors have used the idea of such a primitive sense of self to explain how infants are able to understand the minds of fellow human beings, to develop empathy for others, and eventually to acquire full-fledged self-consciousness. In this scenario, all forms of mature self-consciousness are understood as derivatives of a more primitive and irreducible type of self-awareness.

"The prospect of identifying a core self, or core being without reference to beliefs seems to me incoherent. (Actually the very idea of a core self is terribly fraught in itself.) How does one determinately specify one's individual being? If it is by reactive responses, how does one identify the content of those responses?" The philosopher Robert Pippin's remarks (private communication, August 11, 2018) stem from a long-standing Kantian tradition that identifies selfhood with the possession of concepts and beliefs as held by rational human beings in the form of an "I think" that accompanies all our representations. The position is one that treats as riddled with theoretical-conceptual difficulties claims for the existence of a self that do not include considerations of language, thinking, and belief. Indeed, in the grammatical spirit of Wittgenstein, the philosopher Elizabeth Anscombe denied that the word "I" refers to anything substantive at all, whether mind or body or self, because it is not a referring expression but a first-person utterance. The argument implies that once we humans have understood what it is to master the semantics or grammar of the first-person pronoun, we will have grasped everything that is distinctive about self-reference, and that accordingly the attribution of selfhood to nonlanguage speaking animals is a mistake (Anscombe 1975). The philosopher John McDowell, also on Wittgensteinian grounds, has rejected Anscombe's position by situating self-consciousness in the wider context of his neo-Kantian account of "second nature." According to him, the idea of a persisting self that figures in the continuity of consciousness is not merely formal but can be equated with the continuity of the thinking and perceiving animal that we humans are. Nevertheless, McDowell accepts the neo-Kantian idea that it only makes sense to speak of self-awareness in the case of embodied human beings endowed with the capacity for language and beliefs (McDowell 1996, 99–107).

But Meltzoff and Moore and other researchers in developmental psychology, as well as many other scholars, have tended to reject, downplay, or ignore these considerations. Instead, they have embarked on numerous attempts to specify the conditions determining the emergence of selfhood in infancy and indeed, as we shall see, in nonhuman animals as well. Thus, fundamental to the idea of neonatal imitation has been the notion that newborns possess a primordial awareness of themselves as distinct beings, enabling them from the moment of birth to differentiate between themselves and other humans. As we have seen, Piaget and other earlier figures in developmental psychology had suggested that at birth infants lack an experience of such differentiation. For these authors, the development of self-awareness only occurs at the age of about two years, when infants start to recognize themselves in a mirror or other symbolic device capable of providing an external image or representation of themselves – at the time of the so-called "mirror stage." But Meltzoff and Moore have argued that the neonate's ability to imitate demonstrates that it already possesses an awareness of its difference from others. More precisely, they have proposed that the newborn enjoys a primitive sense of the other as "like" itself (or itself as "like" the other) *and* as sufficiently different from the other that a comparison can be made.

What is at stake in claims for the existence of a sense of self based on newborn imitation? It is precisely the question of the *identity* of the self and others. In a 1993 discussion of the infant's sense of self, the well-known infant researcher Colwyn Trevarthen stated that: "The core of every human consciousness appears to be an immediate, unrational, unverbalized, conceptless, totally atheoretical potential for rapport of the self with another's mind" (Trevarthen 1993, 121). Trevarthen's use of the term "rapport" to describe the relationship between the baby's "self" and that of another might be taken to imply that he had in mind a psychical form of *identification* since, in the past, the word "rapport" had been used to describe the process of psychical identification. Thus, Freud and others in the psychoanalytic tradition had theorized identification as involving an imitative, suggestive-unconscious or quasi-hypnotic merger between the self and another.[22] But for Trevarthen and many other theorists of the self in the

[22] See Leys 2000, chapters 1 and 4, for a discussion of the tension in Freud's theorization of trauma, between a mimetic approach to trauma involving an absorptive mimetic-hypnotic identification with, or imitation of, the aggressor; and an anti-mimetic approach which denies the hypnotic-

postwar period, including Meltzoff and Moore, imitation had little to do with identification in this psychoanalytic or psychic-suggestive sense. Those days were long past. Instead, imitation now tended to refer to the infant's movements and behaviors of the kind that lent themselves to objective observation and experimental controls (for this reason infant imitations were sometimes called "motor imitations") (Meltzoff 2005, 55).

And one consequence of neonatal imitation was held to be the production of a primitive sense of the identity of self and other. "One of the psychological functions that early imitation subserves is to identify people," Meltzoff and Moore observed in 1992 (Meltzoff & Moore 1992, 479). Again, in 1994: "Our theory is that imitation serves an *identity function*. Infants use imitation as a way of re-identifying and communicating with persons they see before them" (Meltzoff & Moore 1994, 96). Or, as they stated in 1995: "We are proposing that one function early imitation serves for infants is to clarify *who* is in front of them when the identity of the person has been put into doubt (as it may be when a person leaves and a person takes the same place)" (Meltzoff & Moore 1995a, 80; authors' emphasis).[23]

Gone, too, were any discussions of the violence and conflict that were integral to psychoanalytically informed approaches to imitation-identification. Instead, the new theorists of the self emphasized that one of the purposes of imitation was to help the infant develop an unconflicted empathy with others. Imitation theorists thus contributed to the burgeoning literature on the nature and mechanisms of empathy in this period. As Meltzoff observed:

> [I]mitation sets children on a trajectory for learning about the other's mind. The "like-me-ness" of others, first manifest in imitation, is a foundation for more mature forms of social cognition that depend on the felt equivalence between self and other. The Golden Rule, "Treat thy neighbor as thy self" at first occurs in action, through imitation. Without an imitative mind, we might not develop this moral mind. Imitation is the bud, and empathy and moral sentiments are the ripened fruit – born from years of interaction with other people already recognized to be "like me." To the human infant, another person is not an alien, but a kindred spirit – not an "It," but an embryonic "Thou." (Meltzoff 2002, 36)

---

immersive process in favor of positing the victim as an autonomous spectator of the traumatic scene.

[23] I note that, in emphasizing issues of identity and personhood while depreciating the role of concepts and beliefs in early infancy, Meltzoff and other development scientists have contributed to a problematic shift that has occurred in much postwar social science and humanities theorizing, away from questions of meaning and signification in favor of questions concerning the primacy of personal identity and individual differences. For discussions of this topic, see Michaels 2004; Leys 2007; 2017.

On this approach, newborn imitation emerged as a crucial mechanism for producing a form of empathy or sympathy for others, a mechanism that had, however, been purged of any hint of the violence and rivalry that earlier had been associated with unconscious mimesis (Decety & Meltzoff 2011).

At first, Meltzoff and Moore did not embrace the idea that newborns possess a sense of self. Their commitment to the supramodal unity of the representations subserving imitation appears to have made them hesitate to do so, because the model did not allow the newborn to differentiate itself from the model. Thus, at the outset Meltzoff and Moore seemed to regard their supramodal hypothesis as antithetical to a newborn sense of self (Moore & Meltzoff 1978, 157, 173). But as Meltzoff and Moore began to grasp the need for differentiations in the supramodal system of representations in order to prevent a confusion between imitator and imitated, they introduced the idea of distinctions between baby and model that would serve as the basis for "self-perception" as well as action (Meltzoff, 1985b, 28–29). As we have seen, they began to propose that although the representations of the infant's body and that of the adult used the same supramodal "language," those representations "are not confused… [T]he mental code may use a suparamodal 'language,' but the mind is not one differentiated supramodal whole" (Meltzoff & Moore, 1995b, 53). On this basis they argued:

> One interesting consequence of this notion of supramodality is that there is a primordial connection between self and other. The actions of other humans are seen as like the acts that can be done at birth. This innate capacity has implications for understanding people, because it suggests an intrinsic relatedness between the seen bodily acts of others and the internal states of oneself (the sensing and representation of one's own movements). A second implication of young infant's possessing a representation of their own bodies is that it provides a starting point for developing objectivity about themselves. This primitive self-representation of the body may be the earliest progenitor of being able to take perspective on oneself, to treat oneself as an object of thought. (Meltzoff & Moore 1995b, 53–54)

Meltzoff et al.'s claim that the infant's recognition of the similarity between itself and another occurs at birth clashed with the view held by Gordon Gallup, who believed from findings using his influential mirror test (after Darwin's use of it with apes) that the child's ability to recognize itself in a mirror occurs much later in development (for a recent assessment of Gallup's mirror test, see Guenther 2017). Without impugning the interest of Gallup's mirror test, Meltzoff and other neonatal imitation theorists emphasized that self-awareness was present in the infant from the very start. It also followed that according to Meltzoff and others, self-awareness is not a function of first-person thoughts – thoughts, as the philosopher Sebastian Rödl has put it, "whose linguistic expression requires the use of the first person pronoun, 'I'" (Rödl 2007, vii). All that was necessary was the infant's capacity for imitative communication with other human beings (Meltzoff 1990, 160).

The idea that as a result of neonatal imitation the newborn gains a "Like Me" experience of the other became a staple of publications by Meltzoff and his coauthors. In 1993, Meltzoff and Gopnik observed:

> [T]he bedrock on which a commonsense psychology is constructed is the apprehension that others are similar to the self. Infants are launched on their career of interpersonal relations with the primary perceptual judgement: **"Here is something like me"** ... We propose that infants' primordial "like me" experiences are based on their understanding of bodily movement patterns and postures. Infants monitor their own body movements by the internal sense of proprioception, and can detect cross-modal equivalents between those movements-as-felt and the movements they see performed by others. Indeed, we will suggest that one reason normal infants preferentially attend to other people is the perceptual judgement that those entities are "like me." (Meltzoff & Gopnik 1993, 336; authors' bold)

The "like me" proposal was linked to "theory of mind" claims by suggesting that neonatal imitation is the mechanism by which infants begin to understand the existence of other minds. As Meltzoff wrote in 1990:

> At what point in development and by what mechanism does the infant see the adult as an "other mind" with intentions, thoughts, and emotions? ... One hypothesis would fix the beginning of this development at the age at which children begin to use "internal state" words ... The data reported here, however, suggest that infants may have the tools to make some initial headway on this problem before these first verbalizations, in part through early imitation and the capacities that underlie it . . . Imitation lies at the cross-roads of infants' elaborating a concept of self and of expanding their understanding of the minds and emotions of others. (Meltzoff 1990, 160–62; see also Meltzoff & Brooks, 2001)

The claim was a form of the classical argument from analogy, as Meltzoff and others recognized (Harris 2005, 173; Meltzoff 2007b, 34).

But it is precisely here that we need to raise some questions. Throughout their work on newborn imitation, Meltzoff, Moore, and their colleagues assumed that there is a gap between the individual and other persons, a gap that can only be filled by positing a mechanism or system of internal representations that mediates between them and serves to close that gap. They posited an inner–outer dualism according to which the mind is an internal, private mental state and the body is an extended external substance: we know our own minds through introspection – if we even know that (Gopnik 1994) – but can only know the minds of other people by analogy with, or inference from, their externally observed behavior. As Meltzoff and Gopnik remarked: "Mental states are located inside the skin (or the head or the body), while physical objects, including the bodies of others, are located outside it." On this view an infant's proprioceptive sensations are "not publicly observable, and are private experiences" (Meltzoff & Gopnik 1993, 339). Or as Meltzoff, Gopnik and Repacholi also stated: "[O]ur sensory experience of other people tells us about their movements in space but does not tell us directly about their mental states" (Meltzoff et al.1999, 17).

The idea that we lack direct knowledge of other minds and hence need mechanisms to overcome this deficit was central to "theory of mind" debates in the cognitive sciences that became pervasive in the 1980s and 1990s. The claim was that, acting rather like miniature scientists, infants need to make inferences, or develop various "theories" (or methods of simulation) as they develop in order to grasp that other human beings actually do have minds like their own. On the one hand, Meltzoff and Moore's claims about newborn imitation reinforced the tendency in the development field to attribute more and more mental functions to innate processes. On the other hand, imitation researchers posited a limit to innate functions, in the sense that, according to them, newborn cognitive capacities did not yet correspond to those of adults. Those cognitive capacities had to be acquired over time, and the acquisition was defined in distinct stages by the different "theories" the infant developed. The entire approach was marked by the assumption that, as Leudar and Costall have put it in an insightful critique of theory of mind approaches, "[i]n making sense of one another, we need to bridge a gulf between what we can 'directly' experience about other people, and what is going on 'in' their minds" and by the related hypothesis that the presumed gulf between people "can only be crossed by inference, theorizing, simulation or some other kind of 'detour'" (Leudar & Costall 2011, 4).

But such ideas are based on a highly problematic dualism of mind and body. Wittgenstein and others influenced by him have forcefully argued that this picture of the relation between self and other minds is defective. There is no gap between the self and the other, they claimed, in the sense of supposing that there is a private self that knows its own mental states introspectively (and therefore with certainty) but only knows the mind of other persons by analogy, inference, simulation, or some related kind of theorizing (therefore uncertainly) because other persons' minds are private too. According to Wittgenstein in his critique of the idea of private language and the argument from analogy, or according to Gilbert Ryle in his similar discussion of what he called the "Cartesian Myth," there is no need to posit the existence of internal mechanisms or processes whose job is to generate quasi-scientific hypotheses or theories or analogies in order to understand the mental states of others. Under ordinary circumstances, we apprehend that others are in pain or are feeling sad or are acting with particular intentions: no inferences or hypotheses are required. This is not a matter of reducing our knowledge of mental states to behavior, because those states can manifest themselves in many ways – in the case of humans, through linguistic communication, for example. (The philosopher Stanley Cavell notes that Wittgenstein often speaks of criteria as consisting in what someone "says and does" but rarely of "someone's *behavior*"; Cavell 1969, 265.)

Nor does any of this rule out the possibility of uncertainty or error, or dissimulation. For Wittgenstein, uncertainty applies to knowing in general. As Chapman has put the point, according to Wittgenstein "it is only because uncertainty is possible that certainty (or knowing) is also possible" (Chapman 1987, 110). In short, our understanding of each other is a function of our grasp of the total linguistic-actional context and situation. (Something of the full complexity of these issues is visible in Cavell's early essay, "Knowing and Acknowledging," which closes with the sentence "To know you are in pain is to acknowledge it, or to withhold the acknowledgment. – I know your pain the way you do") (Cavell 1969, 266).

For Wittgenstein-inspired critics, then, the solution to the problem of other minds does not depend on the subject's "theorizing," or performing analogies, or taking advantage of an AIM mechanism in order to close the alleged gap in knowledge between her own internal, private mental states and someone else's equally private thoughts and feelings. Rather, what is needed is an account of infant development that rejects such a dualism in favor of an approach that pays close attention to the role of social interaction. For researchers Carpendale and Lewis in 2004, this meant returning to Piaget's insights concerning the origins of social understanding from the infant's starting point of relative nondifferentiation between self, other, and the world. These authors argued that only this approach avoided begging the question of the origins of the self, because the argument that an infant is able to infer the existence of other minds based on an analogy between its behavior and someone else's depends on the baby already having a self with which to compare itself to others.[24]

The main thrust of Carpendale and Lewis's critique was therefore to reject what they described as "individualistic" approaches to child development

[24] For similar complaints that Meltzoff and Moore's "Like Me" hypothesis presupposes the very notion of selfhood the AIM hypothesis was supposed to explain, see Carey, 2009, 188–90 and Peacocke 2014, 46–52. However, neither Carey nor Peacocke have questioned the reality of newborn imitation itself.

associated with theory of mind accounts. Instead, they defended a social-constructionist approach that aimed to provide a close study of the child's emergent understanding of mind in the context of its social interactions. Among their recommendations for a changed research agenda was the need to reintroduce detailed longitudinal, naturalistic observations of parent–child interactions of the kind that had been pioneered by Piaget but had been largely displaced by the requirements of more stringent, but potentially misleading, experimental protocols (Carpendale & Lewis 2004).

But at a time when theories of the self and associated theory of mind approaches were so popular in developmental psychology, many researchers rejected Carpendale and Lewis's proposals. Even sympathetic authors accused them of vagueness in their formulations. The response of many commentators to Carpendale and Lewis's arguments was to continue to defend theory of mind approaches; to complain of the authors' underspecification of the internal cognitive mechanisms or processes that, despite Wittgenstein's arguments, they continued to believe were essential to the development of the infant's understanding of other minds; and to raise a host of other objections (for peer commentary, see Carpendale & Lewis 2004, 96–151). The result was that the dualist assumptions that had been so pervasive in cognitive and developmental psychology remained intact (as noted by Leudar and Costall 2011, 20–21).

Indeed, I suggest that it was precisely in the context of such dualist assumptions that neonatal imitation took on its particular importance. As we have seen, in copying another at birth infants are performing opaque or "nonvisible" imitations. They cannot make a direct visual comparison between their own faces and those of others because they have yet to see their own faces in a mirror. Yet according to neonatal imitation claims, newborns are capable of matching the facial movements they see others perform. They are able to register the movements of a face they see but cannot feel (the facial movements of the other) and reproduce them in ways they can feel but cannot see (their own facial movements). *We might put it that newborn imitation provides an exemplary model of how the problem of other minds can be solved based on the mistaken idea that there is a knowledge gap between the individual's private mind or self and the private minds or selves of others.* Thanks to the existence of the hypothesized AIM mechanism and an innate capacity for imitation, so the argument goes, the newborn is immediately able to bridge the alleged gulf between what it privately feels and the private minds and feelings of others, by copying the latter's publicly observable movements. As Meltzoff and Gopnik put this in 1993, "early imitation is relevant to developing theories of mind because it provides the first, primordial instance of infants' making a connection between the visible world of others and the infant's own internal states, the way they 'feel' themselves to be" (Meltzoff & Gopnik 1993, 337).

Meltzoff and Moore's claims about the origins of the self at birth contributed to a burgeoning literature on the topic from the 1980s onwards. An influential paper by Ulric Neisser in 1988 helped give neonatal imitation an important place in such discussions by proposing that there are several kinds of self, of which one crucial kind – the interpersonal self – is the self described by Meltzoff and Moore (I am drawing on Neisser 1988 for the quotations that follow). Thus, Neisser distinguished between five different selves: the most primitive or basic "ecological self," followed in terms of development by the "interpersonal self," the "extended self," the "private self," and finally the "conceptual self." He argued that these several selves are not usually felt as separate, but that nevertheless each self has a distinct origin in terms of the kinds of information on which it is based, its history, and even its pathology.

Inspired in part by Gibson's ideas about the nature of perception, Neisser posited that the most primitive self – the ecological self – is the product of the optical flow of information, combined with the individual's awareness of information provided by its own agency and proprioception in the performance of its embodied, coordinated movements. Based on empirical studies of infant perception, Neisser claimed that by the age of three months the ecological self is more or less complete, so that the infant perceives much the same world as adults do. As he wrote: "The information that specifies the ecological self is omnipresent, and babies are not slow to pick it up … The old hypothesis that a young infant cannot tell the difference between itself and the environment, or between itself and its mother, can be decisively rejected. The ecological self is present from the first." On this basis he vetoed the idea that because children cannot recognize themselves in a mirror until they are about two years old, they have no sense of self until that time. In his view, what children achieve at two years is an understanding of the optics and affordances of mirrors (Neisser drew attention in this connection to an interesting paper on this topic by Loveland 1986). But, he argued, "the ecological self is present much earlier." He claimed that not only humans but all animals whose perceptual systems pick up self-specifying information have some sort of awareness of their ecological selves, though not in the form of conscious self-representations. Those representations only appear in the extended, private, and conceptual selves; "The ecological self, in contrast, is directly perceived."

As for the "interpersonal self," according to Neisser it is the self engaged in "immediate unreflective social interaction with another person," a self that can, like the ecological self, be directly perceived on the basis of objective information. In this case the information comes into play only when two (or more) persons are engaged in interaction – that is, when under appropriate conditions they jointly create intersubjectivity. Neisser stressed that the kind of understanding he attributed to young humans in such intersubjective communication was not intellectual or conceptual: "their interactions do not necessarily involve a conceptual self or a conceptual other." Rather, their engagements with other persons depended on direct perception of the kind observed in Colwyn Trevarthen's studies of "primary intersubjectivity" and Daniel Stern's account of "vitality affects" or "affective attunement" – forms of mutual emotional resonance that occur between infant and others in their daily interactions (Trevarthen 1983; Stern 1985). As Neisser observed of this kind of interpersonal understanding, "The information that specifies vitality affects is directly available in the optic array (and in the acoustic and haptic arrays), and anybody with the right kind of perceptual system can pick it up … That is why even very young infants can perceive and respond appropriately to the affective gestures of other people." And in an acknowledgment of the findings of Meltzoff and Moore he added in a note: "The fact that even newborn infants can apparently imitate facial expressions (Meltzoff & Moore, 1983) provides further support for this view."

Neisser's ideas were taken up and elaborated by numerous theorists of the self (see, for example, Neisser 1993). Claims for the existence of an ecological self were advocated not only by developmental psychologists influenced by Gibson's ideas, but notably by philosophers such as José Luis Bermúdez and others who, starting in the 1990s, began to take an active role in debates over the nature of the self. (Bermúdez has also figured in debates over the nonconceptual content of perception, a topic I discuss in the next section.) An important publication in this regard was *The Body and the Self* (1995), edited by Bermúdez, research scientist Anthony Marcel, and philosopher Naomi Eilan, a collection of articles by a variety of scholars on the topic of the role of the body in the development of the self. In the introductory chapter the editors provided a survey, starting with Descartes, of the complex issues at stake in discussions of self-consciousness and self-awareness. One focus of the collection was whether representing oneself as an object (or self) that persists in time requires only our ability to introspectively acquire knowledge of our own mental states (the "I as subject" thesis), or is only possible when the body is also represented (Bermúdez, Marcel & Eilan 1995, 1–42).

The philosopher Gareth Evans was also an influential figure in this development because, in his discussion of self-identification in his posthumously published *Varieties of Reference* (1982), he emphasized the role of experiences that are "immune to error through misidentification relative to the first person" (Evans 1982, 220–21). By this Evans meant the ways in which we cannot be confused about our ownership of bodily properties of the kind we experience when we cross our legs or have related bodily movements. Evans therefore suggested that our experience of the self derives not only from our mental states but also our bodily experiences, and on this basis challenged the Cartesian conception of the self as an immaterial ego.

Encouraged by these developments, many authors went on to stress bodily awareness in the development of the earliest form of selfhood– what Neisser had labeled the "ecological self" – by tracing its origins back to the newborn's proprioceptive experiences. Here Bermúdez played a prominent role, arguing in line with Neisser's views, which exerted a decisive influence on his thinking, the centrality of proprioception in the development of the infant's ecological self. Evans's claim that proprioception is immune to error through misidentification led Bermúdez to suggest that proprioception counts as an experience of self-awareness prior to the development of language or concepts (Bermúdez 1995, 153–73). Of course, such suggestions were criticized by some researchers and scholars, and there was considerable disagreement as to how best to proceed in this contested area of discussion. But it was in the context of this rapidly expanding work on the self and the body in the 1990s and afterwards that Meltzoff and Moore's ideas gained further traction. Thanks to their paper in Bermúdez et al.'s *The Body and the Self* (Meltzoff & Moore 1995b), as well as their numerous other publications, the idea that newborns can imitate at birth became a staple of discussions of the development of the self – in particular the development of the "interpersonal self." The idea of neonatal imitation provided such a convenient solution to the question of how a baby acquires an "interpersonal self" and can know the minds of others that it was rapidly assimilated into the literature on infant development.

The influence of such claims at this time is evident in the fact that, a year after the appearance of *The Body and the Self*, the phenomenologist Shaun Gallagher joined forces with Meltzoff to coauthor a paper on the self in which neonatal imitation played a prominent role (Gallagher & Meltzoff 1996; see also Gallagher & Marcel 1999; Gallagher 2001). Gallagher responded with enthusiasm to Meltzoff and Moore's newborn imitation studies, declaring them "amazing," and used them to confirm the idea that the newborn possesses a primitive form of self-consciousness (Gallagher 1996, 133). In a 2005 book Gallagher chose the phenomenon of neonatal imitation to introduce his discussion of the role of bodily experience in shaping the mind and the development of a sense of self. Aligning his work with embodied cognition approaches to mindedness that he associated with the work of Bermúdez, Antonio Damasio, Francisco Varela, Evan Thompson, Andy Clark, and others, he stated at the outset of his book:

> The infant, minutes after birth, is capable of imitating the gesture that it sees on the face of another person. It is thus capable of a certain kind of movement that foreshadows intentional action, and that propels it into a human world … Movement and the registration of that movement in a developing proprioceptive system (that is, a system that registers its own self-movement) contributes to the self-organizing development of neuronal structures responsible not only for motor action, but for the way we come to be conscious of ourselves … Across the Cartesian divide, movement prefigures the lines of intentionality, gesture formulates the contours of social cognition, and, in both the most general and most specific ways, embodiment shapes the mind. (Gallagher 2005, 1)

Gallagher also accepted the idea that newborn imitation involved unified intermodal codes requiring no "translation" between modalities while at the same time causing no confusion between self and other. He rejected the tradition associated with works by Merleau-Ponty, Piaget, and others who had regarded the development of a body schema, body image, and primitive forms of self-consciousness as the product of learning and experience. In the same work Gallagher also appealed to the phenomenon of neonatal imitation in order to answer in the affirmative Molyneux's question of whether a person born blind who had learned to discriminate between two shapes by touch alone could, if vision was later restored, immediately identify those shapes by sight alone. "[W]hat I take to be the most secure empirical data, the evidence for neonatal imitation and other experiments on intermodal perception, point to a positive answer for the Molyneux question," he wrote (Gallagher 2005, 80–81, 163).[25]

Similar views have been expressed by the phenomenologist Dan Zahavi, who has made use of claims for neonatal imitation in several of his discussions of selfhood. Throughout his career Zahavi has defended the idea that, in spite of the anti-naturalism of transcendental phenomenology, it is possible to reconcile phenomenology with the project of naturalizing the philosophy of mind. He has maintained that such a reconciliation can be achieved by pursuing a "phenomenological psychology" that, unlike transcendental phenomenology, permits the investigation of consciousness "for its own sake," as opposed to investigating it as a condition of possibility for meaning and truth (Zahavi 2004). On this basis, he has argued for the existence of a primordial consciousness of the self as an intrinsic component of the "first-personal givenness" of experience. Appealing to findings in developmental psychology, he has defended the idea of a core self

[25] In reference to the Molyneux question, Gallagher suggested that although in theory newly sighted persons should pass the Molyneux test, in practice they would fail the test because of the likely deterioration of the nervous apparatus over time (Gallagher 2005, chapter 7). In fact, newly sighted people are flummoxed at first seeing, and only over time can appreciate what they see.

based on the infant's awareness of its earliest engagements with its environment, and hence well before the development of linguistic competence and the use of "I" thoughts (Zahavi 2002).

Like Meltzoff and Moore, Butterworth, Neisser, Bermúdez, Gallagher and others, Zahavi has denied that infants are born into a state of undifferentiation or "fusion" with the mother and world and only gradually develop a sense of the difference between inside and outside. Rather, he has suggested that, thanks to their immediate capacity for perception, their rooting responses, and their ability to imitate, neonates possess a primordial, prereflective, awareness of themselves and an interpersonal understanding that allows them to detect the similarities and differences between themselves and others. According to him, the fact that infants preferentially attend to people rather than objects suggest that they sense others are "like" themselves, just as the fact that they are able to match their imitations to those of others indicate that they have a sense of their bodies as distinct from those of others (Zahavi 2008, 208–213).

It is beyond the scope of this analysis to evaluate in detail Zahavi's arguments about the nature of self-consciousness. In objecting to both Gallagher's and Zahavi's views about the self, some critics have drawn attention to the problematic status of the experiments on neonatal imitation (for criticisms of Gallagher's views, see Welsh 2006; for a reply to Welsh, see Lymer 2014). Until recently, neither Gallagher nor Zahavi appear to have been troubled by such criticisms; both have continued to cite claims for neonatal imitation in their publications. But in 2017, as we have seen, Gallagher intervened in the debate precipitated by Oostenbroek et al.'s 2016 negative evaluation of Meltzoff and Moore's findings by suggesting, with coauthor Vincini and others, that if neonatal imitation is observed at all, it is the byproduct of learned associations and, as such, largely an artifact of experimental conditions.

It is an interesting question to what extent Gallagher and Zahavi's views about the nature of the self would be damaged if it turned out that their confidence in the claims for neonatal imitation had been misplaced. They have made the idea of newborn imitation an important – and in Gallagher's case especially, a central – component of their arguments about the nature of selfhood. In particular, along with many others they have emphasized the special importance of newborn imitation in establishing the infant's "interpersonal" self, to use Neisser's term. It would certainly weaken their arguments if neonatal imitation turned out to be a chimera.

Nevertheless, it seems likely to me that, should they have to abandon the idea of neonatal imitation, they will not discard their theoretical-philosophical views about the existence of a primordial neonatal awareness of the self. Their commitment to the idea of newborn self-consciousness appears to take priority over any particular piece of empirical evidence they are able to adduce in its favor (Zahavi 2014, chapter 4). "[P]henomenal consciousness must be interpreted precisely as entailing a minimal or thin form of self-awareness," Zahavi has observed; "On this account, an experience that lacks self-awareness is nonconscious" (Zahavi 2008, 16). He therefore seems to believe that conscious experience inherently entails consciousness of the self: for him, the attribution of awareness of the self to newborn infants and nonhuman animals appears to be less a phenomenological argument about the inferred nature of their actual experiences (inferred because of course young infants and nonhuman animals cannot testify to their states of awareness) than a supposition about the constitutive nature of prereflective, prelinguistic consciousness.[26]

Be that as it may, it appears that Zahavi's and presumably Gallagher's founding commitments to the very idea of a primitive sense of self-awareness mean that, if they can no longer appeal to neonatal imitation as evidence for such self-awareness, they will not miss it. Claims for an innate capacity for imitation at birth provide useful empirical evidence for assertions about the existence of a core self characterized by self-awareness. But presumably other evidence could take its place, such as evidence of newborn proprioceptive experience or early rooting behavior, without the need for any theoretical adjustments. Bermúdez and other philosophers may make similar adjustments to salvage their ideas about the existence of the self at birth. Meltzoff, Moore, and other psychologists committed to the idea of newborn imitation, however, would be in a more difficult situation if newborn imitation turned out to be a chimera, because their claims for the existence of a primitive or core sense of self at birth based on an innate mimetic capacity would have to be abandoned.

This leaves one further theoretical issue at stake in the idea of neonatal imitation that remains to be discussed – namely, the issue of the nonconceptual nature of perception. We have seen that Bermúdez has made Meltzoff and Moore's perspective central to his ideas about the origins of selfhood. But Bermúdez's interest in neonatal imitation is also important to another question, especially in Anglo-American philosophy: whether the capacities of newborns provide evidence not only of the existence of a self at birth but also of the existence of nonconceptual perceptual contents or states. It is to the arguments of Bermúdez and other like-minded philosophers and to what drives their ideas that I now turn.

[26] For critiques of Zahavi's claim that conscious experience necessarily involves self-consciousness, see Lyyra 2009; Praetorius 2009; Schear 2009. For Zahavi's replies to criticisms, see Zahavi 2011; 2013; 2014, 26–30; 2018.

4.4 Neonatal Imitation and the Nonconceptual Content of Perception

An aspect of the neonatal imitation question that has attracted philosophical attention is whether such imitation implies that newborns can form perceptions without the aid of concepts of any kind, since they have yet to acquire language. Neonatal imitation has been taken to provide empirical evidence for the argument that there are forms of perception and self-awareness that do not depend on concepts or beliefs of any kind. This proposal has interested philosophers because of the significance they attach to the idea of nonconceptual mental content.

Already in 1982, developmental psychologist George Butterworth argued in Gibsonian terms that very young babies possess a direct perception of reality without any need for conceptual capacities. He therefore proposed that there might exist information in sensory stimulation to enable the infant to distinguish self from environment and to perceive object permanence and identity before conceptual knowledge had been acquired. According to Butterworth, nonconceptual information is chiefly derived from stimuli in the visual array and the infant's proprioceptive experiences, but he subsequently added neonatal imitation as another important source (Butterworth 1982, 139; see also Butterworth 1999b). Similar claims based on Gibson's ecological ideas about direct perception were made by several other authors. Indeed, the general thrust of development studies at this time was to suggest that very young infants are capable of perceptions and perceptually driven behaviors, such as imitation, that necessarily occur in the absence of conceptual capacities (see e.g., Neisser 1987; 1991). In the same spirit, in 1999 Meltzoff, Gopnik, and Repacholi emphasized that infants possess a sense of self at birth but not a well-formed concept of the self. According to them, the word "me" in the "Like Me" experience of imitation was not tied to the actual word "me" but referred to subpersonal computational processes (Meltzoff et al. 1999, 18, note 1; Meltzoff 2007b; Saby et al. 2012).

Within philosophy the debate on this topic was launched in 1982 when Gareth Evans argued, with reference to Gibson's claims in *The Senses Considered as Perceptual Systems* (1968), that the content of perceptual experience is nonconceptual. Evans observed, in a widely quoted statement:

> The informational states which a subject acquires through perception are *non-conceptual*, or *non-conceptualized*. Judgements *based upon* such states necessarily involve conceptualization: in moving from a perceptual experience to a judgement about the world (usually expressible in some verbal form), one will be exercising basic conceptual skills … The process of conceptualization or judgement takes the subject from his being in one kind

> of informational state (with a content of a certain kind, namely, non-conceptual content) to his being in another kind of cognitive state (with a content of a different kind, namely, conceptual content). (Evans 1982, 47; author's emphasis)

As the philosopher John McDowell has commented, for Evans, "conceptual content first comes into play, in the context of perception, in judgements based on experience. When one forms a judgement on the basis of experience, one moves from non-conceptual content to conceptual content" (McDowell 1996, 47). McDowell does not agree, as we shall see.

Aspects of Evans' views were taken up and further developed by Christopher Peacocke (Peacocke 1992). Other philosophers who, on various grounds, have also advocated the idea of nonconceptual mental content include Fred Dretske, Adrian Cussins, Tim Crane, Susan Hurley, and Athanassios Raftopoulos (Dretske 1981; Cussins 1990; Crane 1992; Hurley 1998; Raftopoulos 2009; see also Gallagher 2000; Guenther 2003). An active figure in this domain has been Bermúdez, who was among the first philosophers to make use of the findings of neonatal imitation to support his arguments. Bermúdez appears to have been alerted to the interest of newborn imitation around 1995 when Meltzoff and Moore contributed a paper on this topic in the volume *The Body and the Self*, edited by himself and others. On the basis of their own and others' findings, including their claims for newborn imitation, Meltzoff and Moore suggested therein that the infant's earliest grasp of objects was not originally conceptual but merely involved the perception of "proto-objects." In his contribution to the same volume, Bermúdez made the case for the notion of a nonconceptual point of view based on Gibson's ideas about ecological perception. From this it followed that the possession of concepts was not a necessary condition for self-awareness in creatures that are capable of experiencing an ecological distinction between their own experiences and those of other organisms or objects in their worlds. Bermúdez appealed to recent research by the developmental psychologist Elizabeth Spelke and others on object perception in very young infants as evidence that they are capable of primitive forms of object representation without possessing concepts. And with reference also to work by Evans, Peacocke, Cussins, and other philosophers, Bermúdez endorsed the Gibsonian idea of mental states that represent the world but do not require the bearer of those states to possess the relevant concepts. No special argument was needed, he suggested, to demonstrate that "it is possible to have a non-conceptual point of view" because "such a nonconceptual point of view is built into the very structure of perception" (Bermúdez 1995, 153, 155–56, 159).

In 1996, Bermúdez made his first reference to neonatal imitation in the context of a debate over the moral significance of birth. He appealed to

Meltzoff and Moore's findings in order to defend the idea that there is a radical discontinuity between the unborn fetus and the newborn. Arguing that the neonate possesses capacities that fetuses do not, such as a primitive self-awareness, he briefly discussed Meltzoff and Moore's key experiments on newborn imitation, as well as those of Field et al. on the imitation of emotional expressions. Accepting the idea that those experiments supported a "drastic revision" of the traditional Piagetian view of neonates as lacking any sense of a differentiation between themselves and the world, Bermúdez claimed that a primitive form of nonconceptual self-awareness is operative in neonates. "Of course," he wrote, "the essential self-knowledge in fully fledged self-consciousness is fully conceptual and propositional, whereas in the neonatal case it is closer to knowing-how than to knowing-that, but they are on the same developmental continuum" (Bermúdez 1996, 392).

In subsequent publications, Bermúdez integrated the findings of neonatal imitation into his many discussions of the role of nonconceptual mental content in the development of self-awareness. In 1998 he accorded central importance to the role played by the input of information from the visual array and from somatic proprioception in the development of a primitive nonconceptual ecological or "bodily" self, and to neonatal imitation in the development of a nonconceptual intersubjective or psychological sense of the self. He argued that the evidence provided by Meltzoff and Moore and Field et al. on facial imitation in newborns, as well as related studies by development psychologists such as Daniel Stern and Colwyn Trevarthen, made the case for forms of infant self-consciousness prior to the capacity for linguistic mastery and concept formation (Bermúdez 1998). He repeated these arguments in numerous other texts.

It is striking that, so far as I am aware, Bermúdez and other philosophers who have made use of Meltzoff and Moore's work have not voiced any skepticism about the latter's claims. They have not cited the literature questioning the validity of the experimental findings, but appear to have accepted at face value Meltzoff and Moore's assurances that the critiques had been satisfactorily answered. Why is this? What has motivated Bermúdez and like-minded philosophers to uncritically endorse the idea of neonatal imitation?

In a 2005 book devoted to the thought of Gareth Evans, Bermúdez remarked that "Peacocke shares with Evans … a sense that philosophical accounts of concepts and conceptual abilities must respect psychological facts about how the concepts in question are acquired and deployed" (Bermúdez 2005a, 35). And in his own paper in the same publication, Peacocke mentioned Meltzoff and Moore's claims about neonatal imitation as among the "facts" that warranted his views concerning first-person ascriptions (Peacocke 2005, 254–55, and note 21). The trouble is that, as is so often the case in the human sciences, what the "facts" are is open to dispute. But Bermúdez's remarks on Peacocke's commitment to respecting the psychological facts helps foreground one of the features of their work that leads them to be so accommodating to the idea of neonatal imitation. This is the idea that philosophy should take a naturalistic approach to problems in the philosophy of mind and hence should pay close attention to empirical findings. Against philosophers who argue that there is an irreducible difference between truth claims about normative issues versus truth claims in the sciences, Bermúdez proposes instead that the (modern post-Cartesian) natural science paradigm is adequate for self-knowledge. This has led him to argue that philosophers ought to avail themselves of the relevant empirical findings, including especially findings in the psychology of infancy, that throw light on how babies develop self-awareness and cognitive-conceptual capacities (Bermúdez 1999).[27]

Closely intertwined with Bermúdez's arguments in favor of naturalism in the philosophy of mind is his assumption that the so-called "paradox of self-consciousness" renders moot common arguments in favor of a link between human language competence and self-consciousness. According to this paradox, in order to understand self-consciousness it is necessary to employ the very same first-personal propositional judgments or "I" thoughts whose status as such we are trying to explain. As Bermúdez put this in 1998: "The circularity at the heart of the paradox arises from the assumption that the capacity to think thoughts with the first-person contents characteristic of self-consciousness is available only to creatures who have mastered the semantics of the first-person pronoun." This presupposition is a special case of what he calls the Thought-Language Principle, which holds: "The only way to analyze the capacity to think a particular range of thoughts is by analyzing the capacity for the canonical linguistic expression of those thoughts." Rejecting such views, Bermúdez has argued instead that the study of self-consciousness can and ought to be undertaken exclusively from a third-person point of view – namely, that of a scientific observer.[28] Bermúdez's position on this topic relies in turn on the

[27] It is worth noting that it is eminently possible to argue in favor of what has been called a "naïve" or "liberal" naturalism in the philosophy of mind, a naturalism that takes in its stride the idea that forms of mindedness, such as knowing, believing, normative judgments, and intentional mental states are through and through a part of the natural world and not alien or external to it, as post-Cartesian forms of naturalism tend to assume. Such a naïve or liberal naturalism rejects the idea that common-sense psychology must be intelligible from the objective, third-party perspective of the modern natural sciences, a perspective that raises skeptical questions about how to make intelligible our everyday, normative judgments. For critiques of the "traditional" naturalism of the post-Cartesian sciences and defenses of a naïve or liberal naturalism, see McDowell 1994; 2009; Hornsby 1997; and Pippin 2009.

[28] For a rebuttal of this non-circularity argument, as it has been articulated by Peacocke, see McDowell 1996, 162–70.

"Autonomy Principle," according to which "It is possible for a creature to be in states with nonconceptual content, even though that creature possesses no concepts at all." This has allowed Bermúdez to posit the existence of mental states that represent the world "in a way that is independent of concept mastery [as in the case of human infants, who will go on develop concepts] and, moreover, that can be ascribed to creatures who possess no concepts whatsoever [such as nonhuman animals]."

Another of Bermúdez's assumptions is that, according to what he calls the "Acquisition Constraint," it should be possible to show how conceptual capacities observed in human linguistic development can be acquired or derived from nonconceptual perceptions of the kind he believes are shared by human infants and many nonhuman animals alike. "[I]f a given cognitive capacity is psychologically real," he has observed, "then there must be an explanation of how it is possible for an individual in the normal course of human development to acquire that cognitive capacity" (Bermúdez 1998, 43, 13, 61, 83). This means that philosophers must be able to give an account of the origins of conceptual self-consciousness in terms of more primitive, nonconceptual forms of representation and first-person thoughts. In short, Bermúdez proposes that philosophers who share his approach are obliged to try to solve the "interface" problem – namely, how nonconceptual mental content can account for the rational role of perceptual states in the formation of beliefs (Bermúdez 2005b, 171).

A consequence of this last point is that, according to Bermúdez, it ought to be possible to identify continuities between human and nonhuman animals. Against those who see profound differences between humans and other animals in the capacity for conceptuality and rational thought, Bermúdez has sought to identify commonalities. According to him, among those commonalities is the idea that, by virtue of their ability to negotiate their environments and make discriminations of all kinds, nonhuman animals are capable of various degrees of nonconceptual cognitions and simple forms of self-awareness on a par with, and indeed similar in kind to, those of human infants, before the latter develop their distinctive conceptual skills. (He observes in this connection that Peacocke now regards the continuity of infant and animal cognition as the most important argument for the idea that perception has nonconceptual content; Bermúdez & Cahen 2003).

Bermúdez has also supported perceptual nonconceptualism using a "fineness of grain" argument to the effect that perceptual discriminations outstrip our available concepts, thereby justifying the attribution of nonconceptual mental contents in the case of ordinary human perception. The idea is that when, for example, we look at an array of colors of the kind available in paint color samples, our capacity to discriminate the differences between the color samples is finer than any concepts we can bring to bear on them. The argument can be traced back to Gareth Evans, who in 1982 asked: "Do we really understand the proposal that we have as many colour concepts as there are shades of colour that we can sensibly discriminate?" (Evans 1982, 229). Peacocke took up the theme in *A Study of Concepts* (1992) when he proposed that "an experience can often have a finer-grained content than can be formulated by using concepts possessed by the experiencer" (Peacocke 1992, 67). Bermúdez and Cahen have repeated Peacocke's claim, observing that "arguably, I can perceptually discriminate many more colors and shapes than I currently have concepts for" (Bermúdez & Cahen 2003, 7).

Now Bermúdez is aware that several philosophers have raised objections to all of these assumptions. In particular, John McDowell in numerous publications has rejected the idea of nonconceptual perceptual content and has argued instead that human perceptual experience is conceptual through and through. McDowell's is arguably the most influential attempt in recent years to get to grips with the problem of intentionality and mind–world relations by returning to, and building on Kant's and Hegel's treatments of, these topics (Wittgenstein is also an important influence). He forcefully repudiates the idea that it is possible to derive concepts from nonconceptual mental processes of the kind posited by Bermúdez, Peacocke, and many cognitive psychologists. According to McDowell, the key stumbling block is that the arguments of the nonconceptualists fall short of establishing what they need – namely, that nonconceptual content attributable to experiences can constitute a person's reasons for believing something. McDowell's point is that the idea of brute stimuli causally impinging on our senses in the form of nonconceptual impacts "offers exculpations where we wanted justifications." By this he means that nonconceptual, causal accounts of perception of the kind advocated by Bermúdez and others cannot themselves generate the normative concepts on which our evaluative judgments are based (McDowell 1996, 8). Thus, for McDowell the "interface" problem cannot be solved, as Bermúdez thinks it can, by trying to derive concepts from nonconceptual states. For him, it follows that, as he has put it in the neo-Kantian language he deploys, "We must see our way to not needing to give an account of how concepts and intuitions [sensations] are brought into alignment" (McDowell 1994, 205).[29]

[29] For useful discussion of McDowell's views see Matthew Boyle 2012 and 2016. For a critique of Peacocke's efforts to solve the interface problem see Sedivy 1996, 414.

It is an open question whether Bermúdez is right to suggest that although McDowell offers a powerful challenge to defenders of the idea of nonconceptual perceptual content, the latter have the resources to meet it (Bermúdez & Cahen, 2003). It should be clear where my own sympathies lie. But this is not the place to attempt to resolve one of the most difficult issues in contemporary philosophy of mind. My concern, rather, is with the question of what modifications, if any, Bermúdez and other nonconceptual mental content theorists would have to make to their position should they need to abandon neonatal imitation as a basic premise. I surmise that, although the idea of newborn imitation has been attractive to such nonconceptual theorists, it is not so central to their position as to cause them discomfort if it turns out that the evidence is not reliable. They will neither modify nor abandon their theories about nonconceptual mental content but will continue to cite whatever evidence appears to them robust enough in order to defend their views. Given his Gibsonian predelictions, it seems likely to me that if he is obliged to give up claims for newborn imitation, Bermúdez will emphasize instead the idea that self-awareness in the form of an "ecological self" is intrinsic to perception itself, and is accordingly present in the newborn, before it has begun to develop any concepts. Instead of appealing to neonatal imitation, he will cite other evidence of the infant's developing social interactions to explain the origin of the "interpersonal self." Bermúdez's more formidable challenges lie elsewhere – in sustaining his general philosophical claim that it is possible to solve the interface problem by explaining how causally mediated, nonconceptual perceptions are capable of generating normative judgments.

5 Conclusion

It is time to bring my analysis to a close. I began this analysis with the renewed controversy over the existence of neonatal imitation precipitated by Oostenbroek et al.'s impressive 2016 longitudinal study that found no evidence for the phenomenon. The question that has concerned me is what theories built on claims for neonatal imitation would have to be modified or abandoned if it turns out that newborn imitation is an artifact either of methodological complications or the misattribution of infant behavior.

In the process of pursuing this topic, I have suggested that the controversy over newborn imitation can be situated in the context of a number of factors. Those factors include the general post-World War II return to biological and evolutionary approaches in the social and psychological sciences after a period when, chiefly as a result of Nazi racism, such approaches had been treated as taboo, and culturalism had held sway. The renewed biologism of the 1960s and 1970s encouraged a return to claims for the innateness and universalism of certain fundamental psychological processes, as in Chomsky's claims for the existence of a universal grammar and Tomkins' and Ekman's arguments for the universality of the basic emotions. Meltzoff and Moore's claims for the innate character of imitation in newborns and the enthusiastic reception their work received belong to this development. Another, more recent factor is the current replication crisis in the human sciences. Meltzoff and Moore's experiments are a key example of a canonical experiment under fire in an era when many of psychology's great experiments are failing to replicate.

What makes the topic of neonatal imitation especially interesting in this regard is the weight attached to it in much theorizing about human development. The phenomenon of neonatal imitation may not be unique in psychology in anchoring so many theoretical and philosophical claims, but this is certainly an important fact about it. In my analysis I have examined four theories with considerable psychological and philosophical currency, all of which have made use of the putative evidence of newborn imitation: Meltzoff and Moore's AIM hypothesis, mirror neuron and associationist theories of imitation, theories of the self, and theories of the nonconceptual content of perception.

Of these four theories, I have suggested that, if it turns out that newborn imitation is disproven, the last two theories will have to be modified. Advocates of theories of the self and of nonconceptual perception who have made use of claims for neonatal imitation to bolster their views will have to scale back or discard those claims. But I do not believe that the authors will have to forfeit their respective theoretical views, based as they are on prior intellectual-philosophical commitments that require empirical support but can do without the specific support of neonatal imitation. It is hard to predict exactly how those theorists will adjust their arguments, and the adjustments may be painful. But adjust they will.

As for advocates of the AIM hypothesis or its competitors, mirror neuron or AST theorists, they are in a more vulnerable position. If it turns out that neonatal imitation is illusory, then the alternative mirror neuron or associationist theories designed to explain that illusion will be rendered superfluous, although such theories can of course be put to other purposes, as when mirror neurons are used to explain empathy, or when the Association by Similarity Theory is used, persuasively or not, to explain associations other than neonatal imitative matches. But for the discoverers –and, it has to be said, promoters – of neonatal imitation the situation is more dire: the collapse of their empirical claims would undo a lifetime's work and require the abandonment of the AIM hypothesis designed to explain those claims as well as the relinquishment of anti-Piagetian ideas about the innate origins of the self and early social cognition. The AIM hypothesis, as I have tried to show, has in any case has been defective from the start.

References

Anisfeld, M. (1991). Neonatal Imitation. *Developmental Review*, 11 (1), 60–97.

Anisfeld, M. (2005). No Compelling Evidence to Dispute Piaget's Timetable of the Development of Representational Imitation in Infancy. In S. Hurley and N. Chater, eds., *Perspectives on Imitation: From Neuroscience to Social Science, Vol II*. Cambridge, MA: The MIT Press, pp. 107–31.

Anscombe, A. (1975). The First Person. In S. Guttenplan, ed., *Mind and Language*. Oxford: Clarendon Press, pp. 45–65.

Bard, K. A. & Russell, C. L. (1999). Evolutionary Foundations of Imitation: Social, Cognitive and Developmental Aspects of Imitative Processes in Non-Human Primates. In J. Nadel and V. Butterworth, eds., *Imitation in Infancy*. Cambridge: Cambridge University Press, pp. 89–123.

Bargh, J. A. (2011). Unconscious Thought Theory and Its Discontents: A Critique of the Critiques. *Social Cognition*, 29 (6), 629–47.

Bargh, J. A. & Chartrand, T. L. (1999). The Unbearable Automaticity of Being. *American Psychologist*, 54 (7), 462–79.

Barrett, L. F., Adolphs, R., Martinez, S. & Pollak, S. D. (2019). Emotional Expressions Reconsidered: Challenges to Inferring Emotion from Human Facial movements. *Psychological Science in the Public Interest*, 20 (1), 1–68. https://doi:10.1177/1529100619832930

Bellin, H. (1971). The Development of Physical Concepts. In T. Mischel, ed., *Cognitive Development and Epistemology*. New York and London: Academic Press, pp. 85–119.

Berg, E. A. (1948). A Simple Objective Technique for Measuring Flexibility in Thinking. *Journal of General Psychology*, 39 (1), 15–22.

Bermúdez, J. L. (1995). Ecological Perception and the Notion of a Nonconceptual Point of View. In J. L. Bermúdez, A. Marcel, and N. Eilan, eds., *The Body and the Self*. Cambridge, MA: The MIT Press, pp. 153–73.

Bermúdez, J. L. (1996). The Moral Significance of Birth. *Ethics*, 106 (1), 378–403.

Bermúdez, J. L. (1998). *The Paradox of Self-Consciousness*. Cambridge, MA: The MIT Press.

Bermúdez, J. L. (1999). Psychologism and Psychology. *Inquiry*(3–4), 42, 487–504.

Bermúdez, J. L. (2005a). Introduction. In J. L. Bermúdez, ed., *Thought, Reference and Experience: Themes from the Philosophy of Gareth Evans*. Oxford: Oxford University Press, pp. 1–41.

Bermúdez, J. L. (2005b). *Philosophy of Psychology: A Contemporary Introduction*. New York and London: Routledge.

Bermúdez, J. L. & Cahen, A. (2003; revised 2015). Nonconceptual Mental Content. *Stanford Encyclopedia of Philosophy*. https://plato.stanford.edu/entries/content-nonconceptual/notes.html

Bermúdez, J. L., Marcel, A. & Eilan, N. (1995). Self-Consciousness and the Body: An Interdisciplinary Introduction. In J. L. Bermúdez, A. Marcel, and N. Eilan, eds., *The Body and the Self*. Cambridge, MA: The MIT Press, pp. 1–42.

Bower, T. G. R. (1971). The Object in the World of the Infant. *Scientific American*, 225 (4), 30–38.

Bower, T. G. R. (1974a). *Development in Infancy*. San Francisco: W. H. Freeman & Company.

Bower, T. G. R. (1974b). The Evolution of Sensory Systems. In R. B. McLeod and H. L. Pick, eds., *Essays in Honor of J. J. Gibson*. New York: Cornell University Press, pp. 141–51.

Bower, T. G. R. (1976). Repetitive Processes in Child Development. *Scientific American*, 235, 38–47.

Bower, T. G. R. (1977). *A Primer of Infant Development*. San Francisco: W. H. Freeman and Company.

Bower, T. G. R. (1978). Perceptual Development: Object and Space. In E. C. Carterette and M. Friedman, eds., *Vol VIII of Handbook of Perception*. New York: Academic Press, pp. 83–103.

Bower, T. G. R. (1989a). *The Rational Infant: Learning in Infancy*. New York: W. H. Freeman & Company.

Bower, T. G. R. (1989b). The Perceptual World of the Newborn Child. In A. Slater and G. Bremner, eds., *Infant Development*. Hove, UK; Hillsdale, USA: Lawrence Erlbaum, pp. 85–96.

Bower, T. G. R., Broughton, J. M. & Moore, M. K. (1970a). Demonstration of Intention in the Reaching Behavior of Neonate Humans. *Nature*, 228, 679–81.

Bower, T. G. R., Broughton, J. M. & Moore, M. K. (1970b). The Coordination of Vision and Tactual Input in Infancy. *Attention, Perception and Psychophysics*, 8 (1), 51–58.

Boyle, M. (2012). Essentially Rational Animals. In G. Abel and J. Conant, eds., *Vol. II of Rethinking Epistemology*. Berlin: Walter de Gruyer, pp. 395–427.

Boyle, M. (2016). Additive Theories of Rationality: A Critique. *European Journal of Philosophy*, 24 (3), 527–55.

Brass, M. & Heyes, C. (2005). Imitation: Is Cognitive Neuroscience Solving the Correspondence Problem? *Trends in Cognitive Sciences*, 9 (10), 489–95.

Burman, E. (2017). *Deconstructing Developmental Psychology*, 3rd ed., London and New York: Routledge, pp. 39–41.

Bushnell, W. R. (1998). The Origins of Face Perception. In F. Simion and G. Butterworth, eds., *The Development of Sensory, Motor and Cognitive Capacities in Early Infancy.* Hove, Sussex: Psychology Press Ltd., pp. 69–84.

Butterworth, G. (1982). Object Permanence and Identity in Piaget's Theory of Infant Cognition. In G. Butterworth, ed., *Infancy and Epistemology: An Evaluation of Piaget's Theory.* New York: St. Martin's Press, pp. 137–69.

Butterworth, G. (1999a). Neonatal Imitation: Existence, Mechanisms and Motives. In J. Nadel and G. Butterworth, eds., *Imitation in Infancy.* Cambridge: Cambridge University Press, pp. 63–88.

Butterworth, G. (1999b). A Developmental-Ecological Perspective on Strawson's "The Self." In S. Gallagher and J. Shear, eds., *Models of the Self.* Charlottesville: Imprint Academic, pp. 203–11.

Calvert, G., Spence, C. & Stein, B. E., eds. (2004). *The Handbook of Multisensory Processes*. Cambridge, MA: The MIT Press.

Carey, S. (2009). *The Origin of Concepts*. Oxford: Oxford University Press.

Carpendale, J. I. M. & Lewis, C. (2004). Constructing an Understanding of Mind: The Development of Children's Understanding Within Social Interaction. *Behavioral and Brain Sciences*, 27 (1), 79–96, peer commentary, 96–151.

Catmur, C., Walsh, V. & Heyes, C. (2007). Sensorimotor Learning Configures the Human Mirror System. *Current Biology*, 17, 1527–31.

Cavell, S. (1969). *Must We Mean What We Say? A Book of Essays*. New York: Charles Scribner's Sons.

Chapman, M. N. (1987). Inner Processes and Outward Criteria: Wittgenstein's Importance for Psychology. In M. Chapman and R. A. Dixon, eds., *Meaning and the Growth of Understanding: Wittgenstein's Significance for Developmental Psychology.* Berlin: Springer-Verlag, pp. 103–27.

Chartrand, T. L. & Bargh, J. A. (1999). The Chameleon Effect: The Perception-Behavior Link and Social Interaction. *Journal of Personality and Social Psychology*, 76 (6), 893–910.

Chartrand, T. L., Maddux, W. W. & Lakin, J. L. (2005). Beyond the Perception-Behavior Link: The Ubiquitous Utility and Motivational Moderators of Nonconscious Mimicry. In R. R. Hassin, J. E. Uleman, and J. A. Bargh, eds., *The New Unconscious*. Oxford: Oxford University Press, pp. 334–61.

Chomsky, N. (1968). *Language and Mind.* New York: Harcourt.

Costall, A. & Leudar, I. (2004). Where is the "Theory" in Theory of Mind? *Theory and Psychology*, 14(5), 623–46.

Coulter, J. (1982). Theoretical Problems in Contemporary Cognitive Science. *Inquiry*, 25 (1), 3–36.

Coulter, J. (1985). Two Concepts of the Mental. In K. J. Gergem and K. Davis, eds., *The Social Construction of the Person*. New York: Springer-Verlag, pp. 130–44.

Coulter, J. (1987). Recognition in Wittgenstein and Contemporary Thought. In M. Chapman and R. A. Dixon, eds., *Meaning and the Growth of Understanding: Wittgenstein's Significance for Developmental Psychology*. Berlin: Springer-Verlag, pp. 85–102.

Coulter, J. (2008). Twenty-Five Theses Against Cognitivism. *Theory Culture Society*, 25(2), 19–32.

Coulter, J. & Sharrock, W. (2007). *Brain, Mind and Human Behavior in Contemporary Cognitive Science: Critical Assessments of the Philosophy of Psychology*. Lewiston: Edwin Mellen Press.

Crane, T. (ed). (1992). The Non-Conceptual Content of Experience. *The Contents of Experience*. Cambridge: Cambridge University Press, pp. 136–58.

Crivelli, C. & Fridlund, A. J. (2018). Facial Displays are Tools for Social Influence. *Trends in Cognitive Sciences*, 22 (5), 388–99.

Crivelli, C., Jarillo, S., Russell, J. A. & Fernández-Dols, J. M. (2016a). Reading Emotions from Faces in Two Indigenous Societies. *Journal of Experimental Psychology: General*, 145 (7), 830–43.

Crivelli, C., Russell, J. A., Jarillo, S. & Fernández-Dols, J. M. (2016b). The Fear Gasping Face as a Threat Display in a Melanesian society. *Proceedings of the National Academy of Sciences USA*, 113 (44), 12403–12407.

Cussins, A. (1990). The Connectionist Construction of Concepts. In M. Boden, ed., *The Philosophy of Artificial Intelligence*. Oxford: Oxford University Press, pp. 368–440.

Davis, J., Redshaw, J., Suddendorf, T., et al. (2020). Does Neonatal Imitation Exist? Insights from a Meta-Analysis of 336 Effect Sizes. *Perspectives on Psychological Science*, forthcoming.

Decety, J. & Meltzoff, A. N. (2011). Empathy, Imitation, and the Social Brain. In A. Copland and P. Goldie, eds., *Empathy: Philosophical and Psychological Perspectives*. Oxford: Oxford University Press, pp. 58–81.

Decock, L. & Douven, I. (2011). Similarity After Goodman. *Review of Philosophical Psychology*, 2 (1), 61–75.

Dretske, F. (1981). *Knowledge and the Flow of Information*. Cambridge, MA: The MIT Press.

Dunkeld, J. (1978). *The Function of Imitation in Infancy*. Unpublished doctoral dissertation, University of Edinburgh.

Duran, J. I., Reisenzein, R. & Fernández-Dols, J. M. (2017). Coherence Between Emotions and Facial Expressions. In J. M. Fernández-Dols and J. A. Russell, eds., *The Science of Facial Expression*, 2nd ed. Oxford: Oxford University Press, pp. 107–29.

Ekman, P. & Friesen, W. V. (1971). Constants Across Cultures in the Face and Emotion. *Journal of Personality and Social Psychology*, 17 (2), 124–29.

Evans, G. (1982). *The Varieties of Reference*. Oxford: Oxford University Press.

Field, T. M., Goldstein, S., Vega-Lahr, N., and Porter, K. (1986). Changes in Imitative Behavior During Early Infancy. *Infant Behavior and Development*, 9 (4), 415–21.

Field, T. M., Woodson, R., Cohen, D. et al. (1983). Discrimination and Imitation of Facial Expressions by Term and Preterm Neonates. *Infant Behavior and Development* 6(4), 485–89.

Field, T. M., Woodson, R., Greenberg, R. & Cohen, D. (1982). Discrimination and Imitation of Facial Expressions by Neonates. *Science, New Series*, 218 (4568), 179–81.

Fodor, J. (1975). *The Language of Thought*. Cambridge, MA: Harvard University Press.

Fodor, J. (1981). *Representations: Philosophical Essays on the Foundations of Cognitive Science*. Cambridge, MA: The MIT Press.

Fontaine, R. (1984). Imitative Skill Between Birth and Six Months. *Infant Behavior and Development*, 7(3), 323–33.

Fridlund, A. J. (1994). *Human Facial Expression: An Evolutionary View*. New York: Academic Press.

Fridlund, A. J. (2017). The Behavioral Ecology View of Facial Displays, 25 Years Later. In J. M. Fernández-Dols and J. A. Russell, eds., *The Science of Facial Expression*, 2nd ed. Oxford: Oxford University Press pp. 77–92.

Gallagher, S. (1996). The Moral Significance of Primitive Self-Consciousness. *Ethics*, 107(1), 129–40.

Gallagher, S. (2000). Philosophical Conceptions of the Self: Implications for Cognitive Science. *Trends in Cognitive Sciences*, 4 (1), 14–21.

Gallagher, S. (2001). Emotion and Intersubjective Perception: A Speculative Account. In A. Kaszniak, ed., *Emotions, Qualia, and Consciousness*. River Edge: World Scientific Publishing Co., pp. 95–100.

Gallagher, S. (2005). *How the Body Shapes the Mind*. Oxford: Clarendon Press.

Gallagher, S. & Marcel, A. J. (1999). The Self in Contextualized Action. In S. Gallagher and J. Shear, eds., *Models of the Self*. Charlottesville: Imprint Academic, pp. 273–99.

Gallagher, S. & Meltzoff, A. N. (1996). The Earliest Sense of Self and Others: Merleau-Ponty and Recent Developmental Studies. *Philosophical Psychology*, 9 (2), 211–34.

Gallese, V. (2007). The Two Sides of Mimesis: Mimetic Theory, Embodied Simulation, and Social Identification. In S. R. Garrels, ed., *Mimesis and Science: Empirical Research on Imitation and the Mimetic Theory of Culture and Religion*. East Lansing: Michigan State University Press, pp. 87–108.

Gallese, V., Gernsbacher, M. A., Heyes, C., Hickok, G. & Iacoboni, M. (2011). Mirror Neuron Forum. *Perspectives on Psychological Science*, 6 (4), 369–407.

Gardner, J. & Gardner, H. (1970). A Note on Selective Imitation by a Six-Week Old Infant. *Child Development* 4, 1209–13.

Gendron, M., Roberson, D., van der Vyver, J. M. & Barrett, L. F. (2014). Perceptions of Emotion from Facial Expressions are not Culturally Universal: Evidence from a Remote Culture. *Emotion*, 124 (2), 251–62.

Gibson, E. J. (1969). *Principles of Perceptual Learning and Development*. New York: Appleton-Century-Crofts.

Gibson, E. J. & Walk, R. D. (1960). The Visual Cliff. *Scientific American*, 202 (4), 67–71.

Gibson, J. J. (1966). *The Senses Considered as Perceptual Systems*. New York: Houghton Mifflin Company.

Gibson, J. J. (1986). *The Ecological Approach to Visual Perception*. Hillsdale: Lawrence Erlbaum Associates.

Goodman, N. (1972). Seven Strictures on Similarity. *Problems and Projects*. Indianapolis: Bobbs-Merrill, pp. 437–46.

Gopnik, A. (1994). How We Know Our Minds: The Illusion of First-Person Knowledge of Intentionality. *Behavioral and Brain Sciences*, 16(1), 1–14.

Guenther, K. (2017). Monkeys, Mirrors and Me: Gordon G. Gallup and the Study of Self-Recognition. *Journal of the History of the Behavioral Sciences*, 53 (1), 5–27.

Guenther, Y. H. (2003). *Essays on Nonconceptual Content*. Cambridge, MA: The MIT Press.

Hamlyn, D. W. (1971). Epistemology and Development. In T. Mischel, eds., *Cognitive Development and Epistemology*. New York & London: Academic Press, pp. 3–24.

Hamlyn, D. W. (1978). *Experience and the Growth of Understanding. London*, Boston and Henley: Routledge & Kegan Paul.

Harris, P. L. (2005). Grasping Action. In S. Hurley and N. Chater, eds., *Perspectives on Imitation. From Neuroscience to Social Science, Vol II*. Cambridge, MA: The MIT Press, pp. 173–78.

Hayes, L. A. & Watson, J. S. (1981). Neonatal Imitation: Fact or Artifact? *Developmental Psychology*, 17 (5), 655–60.

Heimann, M. (1999). Notes on Individual Differences and the Assumed Elusiveness of Neonatal Imitation. In A. N. Meltzoff and W. Prinz, eds.,

The Imitative Mind: Development, Evolution, and Brain Bases. Cambridge: Cambridge University Press, pp. 74–84.

Heyes, C. (2005). Imitation by Association. In S. Hurley and N. Chater, eds., *Perspectives on Imitation. Mechanisms of Imitation and Imitation in Animals, Vol I*. Cambridge, MA: The MIT Press, pp. 157–76.

Hickok, G. (2014). *The Myth of Mirror Neurons: The Real Neuroscience of Communication and Cognition*. New York and London: W. W. Norton & Company.

Hornsby, J. (1997). *Simple Mindedness. In Defense of Naïve Naturalism in the Philosophy of Mind*. Cambridge, MA: Harvard University Press.

Hurley, S. (1998). *Consciousness in Action*. Cambridge, MA: Harvard University Press.

Iacobini, M. (2009). Imitation, Empathy, and Mirror Neurons. *Annual Review of Psychology*, 60, 653–670.

James, W. (1890). *The Principles of Psychology*. New York: H. Holt & Company.

Jones, S. (1996). Imitation or Exploration? Young Infants' Matching of Adults' Oral Gestures. *Child Development*, 67 (5), 1952–969.

Jones, S. (2005). The Role of Mirror Neurons in Imitation. In *Perspectives on Imitation. Vol. 1. Mechanisms of Imitation and Imitation in Animals*. Cambridge, MA: The MIT Press, pp. 205–210.

Jones, S. (2006). Exploration or Imitation? The Effect of Music on 4-week-old Infants' Tongue Protrusion. *Infant Behavior and Development*, 29 (1), 126–30.

Jones, S. (2009). The Development of Imitation in Infancy. *Philosophical Transactions of the Royal Society of London. B. Biological Sciences*, 364 (1528), 2325–335.

Jones, S. (2016). Can Newborns Imitate? *WIREs Cognitive Science*, 8 (1–2), e1410. https://doi:10.1002/wcs.1410

Jones, S. (2017). The Case Against Newborn Imitation Grows Stronger. *Behavioral and Brain Sciences*, 40, 27–28. https://doi.org/10.1017/S0140525X16001886

Kaitz, M., Meschulach-Sarfaty, O., Auerbach J. & Eidelman, A. (1988). A Reexamination of Newborns' Ability to Imitate Facial Expressions. *Developmental Psychology*, 24 (1), 3–7.

Kaplan, B. (ed.) (1971). Foreword. *Imitation in Children*. By Paul Guillaume. Chicago: University of Chicago Press, 1971, pp. xv–xvi.

Kennedy-Constantini, S., Oostenbroek, J., Suddendorf, T., et al. (2017). There is No Compelling Evidence that Human Neonates Imitate. *Behavioral and Brain Sciences*, 40, 28–29.

Kessen, W. (1996). American Psychology Just Before Piaget. *Psychological Science*, 7 (4), 196–99.

Keven, N. & Akins, K. A. (2017). Neonatal Imitation in Context: Sensory-Motor Development in the Perinatal Period. *Behavioral and Brain Sciences*, 40, 1–58.

Leudar, I. & Costall, A., eds. (2011). *Against Theory of Mind*. Basingstoke: Palgrave Macmillan Publishers Limited.

Leys, R. (2000). *Trauma: A Genealogy*. Chicago: University of Chicago Press.

Leys, R. (2007). *From Guilt to Shame: Auschwitz and After*. Princeton: Princeton University Press.

Leys, R. (2012). "Both of Us Disgusted in *My* Insula": Mirror Neuron Theory and Emotional Empathy. *nonsite.org*, *#5*. Reprinted in F. Biess and D. Gross, eds., *Science and Emotions After 1945: A Transatlantic Perspective* (2014). Chicago: University of Chicago Press, pp. 67–95.

Leys, R. (2017). *The Ascent of Affect: Genealogy and Critique*. Chicago: University of Chicago Press.

Loveland, K. (1986). Discovering the Affordances of a Reflecting Surface. *Developmental Review*, 6 (2), 1–24.

Lymer, J. (2014). Infant Imitation and the Self. A Response to Welsh. *Philosophical Psychology*, 27 (2), 235–57.

Lyyra, P. (2009). Two Senses for "Givenness of Consciousness." *Phenomenology and the Cognitive Sciences*, 8, 67–87.

Mandelbaum, E. (2015). Associationist Theories of Thought. *Stanford Encyclopedia of Philosophy*. https://plato.stanford.edu/entries/associationist-thought/

Maratos, O. (1973). *The Origin and Development of Imitation in the First Six Months of Life*. Doctoral dissertation, University of Geneva.

Marshall, P. J. & Meltzoff, A. N. (2014). Neural Mirroring Mechanisms and Imitation in Human Infants. *Philosophical Transactions of the Royal Society. Biological Sciences* 369(1644), 20130620. https://dx.doi.org/10.1098/rstb.2013.0620

McDowell, J. (1994). The Content of Perceptual Experience. *The Philosophical Quarterly*, 44 (175), 190–205.

McDowell, J. (1996). *Mind and World*. Cambridge, MA: Harvard University Press.

McDowell, J. (2009). Naturalism in the Philosophy of Mind. *The Engaged Intellect*. Cambridge, MA: Harvard University Press, pp. 257–75.

Meltzoff, A. N. (1982). Imitation, Intermodal Coordination and Representation in Early Infancy. In G. Butterworth, ed., *Infancy and Epistemology: An Evaluation of Piaget's Theory*. New York: St. Martin's Press, pp. 85–114.

Meltzoff, A. N. (1985a). Immediate and Deferred Imitation in Fourteen- and Twenty-Four-Month-Old Infants. *Child Development*, 56 (1), 62–72.

Meltzoff, A. N. (1985b). The Roots of Social and Cognitive Development: Models of Man's Original Nature. In T. M. Field and N. A. Fox, eds., *Social Perception in Infants*. University of Michigan: Ablex Publishing Corporation, pp. 1–30.

Meltzoff, A. N. (1988). The Human Infant as Homo Imitans. In T. R. Zentall and B. G. Galef, eds., *Social Learning: Psychological and Biological Perspectives*. Hillsdale: Lawrence Erlbaum, pp. 319–41.

Meltzoff, A. N. (1990). Foundations for Developing a Concept of Self: The Role of Imitation in Relating Self to Other and the Value of Social Mirroring, Social Modeling, and Self Practice in Infancy. In D. Cicchetti and M. Beeghly, eds., *The Self in Transition: Infancy to Childhood*. Chicago: University of Chicago Press, pp. 139–64.

Meltzoff, A. N. (2002). Elements of a Developmental Theory of Imitation. In A. N. Meltzoff and W. Prinz, eds., *The Imitative Mind: Development, Evolution, and Brain Bases*. Cambridge: Cambridge University Press, pp. 19–41.

Meltzoff, A. N. (2005). Imitation and Other Minds: The "Like Me" Hypothesis. In S. Hurley and N. Chater, eds., *Perspectives on Imitation. From Neuroscience to Social Science, Vol II*. Cambridge, MA: The MIT Press, pp. 55–77.

Meltzoff, A. N. (2007a). "Like Me": A Foundation for Social Cognition. *Developmental Science*, 10 (1), 126–34.

Meltzoff, A. N. (2007b). The "Like Me" Framework for Recognizing and Becoming an Intentional Agent. *Acta Psychologica*, 124 (1), 26–43.

Meltzoff, A. N. (2017). Elements of a Comprehensive Theory of Imitation. *Behavioral and Brain Sciences*, 40, 32–33.

Meltzoff, A. N. & Borton, R. W. (1979). Intermodal Matching by Human Neonates. *Nature*, 282, 403–4.

Meltzoff, A. N. & Brooks, R. (2001). "Like Me" as a Building Block for Understanding Other Minds: Bodily Acts, Attention, and Intention. In B. F. Maille, L. J. Moses, and D. W. Baldwin, eds., *Intentions and Intentionality: Foundations of Social Cognition*. Cambridge, MA: The MIT Press, pp. 171–92.

Meltzoff, A. N. & Decety, J. (2003). What Imitation Tells Us About Social Cognition: A Rapprochement Between Developmental Psychology and Cognitive Neuroscience. *Philosophical Transactions of the Royal Society. B. Biological Sciences*, 358 (1431), 491–500.

Meltzoff, A. N. & Gopnik, A. (1993). The Role of Imitation in Understanding Persons and Developing a Theory of Mind. In S. Baron-Cohen, H. Tager-

Flusberg, and D. J. Cohen, eds., *Understanding Other Minds*. Oxford: Oxford University Press, pp. 335–66.

Meltzoff, A. N. & Moore, M. K. (1977). Imitation of Facial and Manual Gestures by Human Neonates. *Science*, new series, 198 (4312), 75–78.

Meltzoff, A. N. & Moore, M. K. (1983). The Origins of Imitation in Infancy: Paradigm, Phenomena, and Theories. *Advances in Infancy Research*, 2, 265–301.

Meltzoff, A. N. & Moore, M. K. (1989). Imitation in Newborn Infants: Exploring the Range of Gestures and the Underlying Mechanisms. *Developmental Psychology*, 25 (6), 954–62.

Meltzoff, A. N. & Moore, M. K. (1992). Early Imitation Within a Functional Framework: The Importance of Person Identity, Movement, and Development. *Infant Behavior and Development*, 15 (4), 479–505.

Meltzoff, A. N. & Moore, M. K. (1994). Imitation, Memory, and the Representation of Persons. *Infant Behavior and Development*, 17(1), 83–99.

Meltzoff, A. N. & Moore, M. K. (1995a). A Theory of the Role of Imitation in the Emergence of the Self. In P. Rochat, ed., *The Self in Infancy: Theory and Research*. New York: Elsevier, pp. 73–93.

Meltzoff, A. N. & Moore, M. K. (1995b). Infant's Understanding of People and Things: From Body Imitation to Folk Psychology. In J. L. Bermúdez, A. Marcel, and N. Eilan, eds., *The Body and the Self*. Cambridge, MA: The MIT Press, pp. 43–69.

Meltzoff, A. N. & Moore, M. K. (1997). Explaining Facial Imitation: A Theoretical Model. *Early Development and Parenting*, 6 (3–4), 179–92.

Meltzoff, A. N. & Prinz, W. (2002). *The Imitative Mind: Development, Evolution, and Brain Behavior*. Cambridge: Cambridge University Press.

Meltzoff, A. N., Gopnik, A. & Repacholi, B. M. (1999). Toddlers' Understanding of Intentions, Desires, and Emotions: Explorations of the Dark Ages. In P. D. Zelazo, J. W. Astington, and D. R. Olson, eds., *Developing Theories of Intention: Social Underestanding and Self-Control*. Hillsdale: Lawrence Erlbaum, pp. 17–40.

Meltzoff, A. N., Kuhl, P. K. & Moore, M. K. (1991). Perception, Representation, and the Control of Action in Newborns and Infants. Toward a Synthesis. In M. J. Weiss and P. Zelazo, eds., *Newborn Attention: Biological Constraints and the Influence of Experience*. Norwood: Ablex Pub. Corp., pp. 377–411.

Meltzoff, A. N., Murray, L., Simpson, E., et al. (2018). Re-examination of Oostenbroek et al. (2016): Evidence for Neonatal Imitation of Tongue Protrusion. *Developmental Science*, 21 (4), e12609. https://doi.10.1111/desc.12609

Meltzoff, A. N., Murray, L., Simpson, E., et al. (2019). Eliciting Imitation in Early Infancy. *Developmental Science*, 22 (2), e12738. https://doi: 10.1111/desc. 12738

Michaels, W. Benn. (2004). *The Shape of the Signifier. From 1967 to the End of History*. Princeton: Princeton University Press.

Michotte, A. G., Thinès, R. & Crabbé, G. (1964). *Les compléments amodaux des structures perspectives*. Louvain, Belgium: Publications U. Louvain.

Moore, M. K. & Meltzoff, A. N. (1975). Neonate Imitation: A Test of Existence and Mechanism. Paper presented at the meeting of the Society for Research on Child Development, Denver, Colorado.

Moore, K. M. & Meltzoff, A. N. (1978). Object Permanence, Imitation, and Language Development in Infancy: Toward a Neo-Piagetian Perspective on Communicative and Cognitive Development. In F. D. Minifie and L. Lloyd, eds., *Communication and Cognitive Abilities – Early Behavioral Assessment*. Baltimore: University Park Press, pp. 151–84.

Morawski, J. (2019). The Replication Crisis: How Might Philosophy and Theory of Psychology Be of Use? *Journal of Theoretical and Philosophical Psychology*, 39 (4), 218–39.

Morgan, M. J. (1977). *Molyneux's Question: Vision, Touch, and the Philosophy of Perception*. Cambridge: Cambridge University Press.

Nehaniv, C. L. & Dautenhahn, K. (2002). The Correspondence Problem. In K. Dautenhahn and C. L. Nehaniv, eds., *Imitation in Animals and Artifacts*. Cambridge, MA: The MIT Press, pp. 41–61.

Neisser, U. (ed.) (1987). *Concepts and Conceptual Development: Ecological and Intellectual Factors in Categorization*. Cambridge: Cambridge University Press.

Neisser, U. (1988). Five Kinds of Self-Knowledge. *Philosophical Psychology*, 1 (1), 35–59.

Neisser, U. (1991). Two Perceptually Given Aspects of the Self and Their Development. *Developmental Review*, 11(3), 197–209.

Neisser, U. (ed.) (1993). *The Perceived Self: Ecological and Interpersonal Sources of Self-Knowledge*. Cambridge: Cambridge University Press.

Nelson, C. A. (1987). Recognition of Facial Expressions in the First Two Years of Life: Mechanisms of Development. *Child Development*, 58 (4), 889–909.

Oostenbroek, J., Slaughter, V., Nielsen, M. & Suddendorf, T. (2013). Why the Confusion Around Neonatal Imitation? *Journal of Reproductive and Infant Psychology* 31 (4), 328–41. https://doi.org/10.1080/02646838.2013.832180

Oostenbroek, J., Suddendorf, T., Nielsen, M., et al. (2016). Comprehensive Longitudinal Study Challenges the Existence of Neonatal Imitation in Humans. *Current Biology*, 26 (2016), 1334–38. https://doi.org/10.1016/j.cub.2016.03.047

Oostenbroek, J., Redshaw, J., Slaughter, V., et al. (2018). Re-Evaluating the Neonatal Hypothesis. *Developmental Science*, 22 (2), e12720. https://doi.org/10.1111/desc.12720

Parton, D. A. (1976). Learning to Imitate in Infancy. *Child Development*, 47 (1), 14–31.

Peacocke, C. (1992). *A Study of Concepts*. Cambridge, MA: The MIT Press.

Peacocke, C. (2005). "Another I": Representing Conscious States, Perception, and Others. In J. L. Bermúdez, eds., *Thought, Reference and Experience: Themes from the Philosophy of Gareth Evans*. Oxford: Oxford University Press, pp. 220–57.

Peacocke, C. (2014). *The Mirror of the World: Subjects, Consciousness, and Self-Consciousness*. Oxford: Oxford University Press.

Piaget, J. (1953). *The Origin of Intelligence in the Child*. Translated by Margaret Cook. Harmondsworth: Penguin.

Piaget, J. (1954). *The Construction of Reality in the Child*. Translated by Margaret Cook. New York: Ballantine Books.

Piaget, J. (1962). *Plays, Dreams and Imitation in Childhood*. Translated by C. Gattegno & F. M. Hodgson. New York: W. W. Norton & Company.

Piaget, J. (1972). *Principles of Genetic Epistemology*. Translated by Wolfe Mays. London & New York: Routledge.

Piaget, J. & Inhelder, B. (1969). *The Psychology of the Child*. Translated by Helen Weaver. New York: Basic Books.

Piattelli-Palmarini, M. (ed.) (1980). *Language and Learning: The Debate Between Jean Piaget and Noam Chomsky*. Cambridge, MA: Harvard University Press.

Pippin, R. (2009). Natural and Normative. *Daedalus*, 138 (3), 35–43.

Poulson, C. L., de Paula Nunes, L. R. & Warren, S. F. (1989). Imitation in Infancy: A Critical Review. *Advances in Child Development and Behavior*, 22, 271–98.

Praetorius, N. (2009). The Phenomenological Underpinning of the Notion of a Minimal Core Self: A Psychological Perspective. *Consciousness and Cognition*, 18 (3), 325–38.

Prinz, W. (2012). *Open Minds: The Social Making of Agency and Intentionality*. Cambridge, MA: The MIT Press.

Prinz, W. & Meltzoff, A. N. (2002). An Introduction to the Imitative Mind and Brain. In A. N. Meltzoff and W. Prinz, eds., *The Imitative Mind: Development, Evolution, and Brain Bases*. Cambridge: Cambridge University Press, pp. 1–15.

Raftopoulos, A. (2009). *Cognition and Perception: How Do Psychology and Neural Science Inform Philosophy?* Cambridge, MA: The MIT Press.

Ray, E. & Heyes, C. (2011). Imitation in Infancy: The Wealth of the Stimulus. *Developmental Science*, 14 (1), 92–105.

Redshaw, J., Nielsen, M., Slaughter, V., et al. (2020). Individual Differences in Neonatal "Imitation" Fail to Predict Early Social Cognitive Behavior. *Developmental Science*, 23(2), e12892. https://doi.org/10.1111/desc.12892

Rodkey, E. (2015). The Visual Cliff's Forgotten Menagerie: Rats, Goats, Babies, and Myth-Making in the History of Psychology. *Journal of the History of the Behavioral Sciences*, 51 (2), 113–40.

Rödl, S. (2007). *Self-Consciousness*. Cambridge, MA: Harvard University Press.

Ruba, A, L. & Repacholi, B. M. (2019). Do Preverbal Infants Understand Discrete Facial Expressions of Emotion? *Emotion Review*. https://doi .10.1177/1754073919871098

Russell, J. (1979). The Status of Genetic Epistemology. *Journal for the Theory of Social Behavior*, 9(1), 53–70.

Russell, J. (1982). Piaget's Theory of Sensori-Motor Development: Outlines, Assumptions, Problems. In G. Butterworth, ed., *Infancy and Epistemology: An Evaluation of Piaget's Theory*. New York: St. Martin's Press, pp. 3–29.

Russell, J. A. (1994). Is There Universal Expression of Emotions from Facial Expressions? A Review of Cross-Cultural Studies. *Psychological Bulletin*, 115 (1), 102–41.

Saby, J. N., Marshall, P. J. & Meltzoff, A. N. (2012). Neural Correlates of Being Imitated: An EEG Study in Preverbal Infants. *Social Neuroscience*, 7, 650–51.

Schear, J. K. (2009). Experience and Self-Consciousness. *Philosophical Studies*, 144 (1), 95–105.

Sedivy, S. (1996). Must Conceptually Informed Perceptual Experience Involve Non-Conceptual Content? *Canadian Journal of Philosophy*, 26 (3), 413–31.

Simpson, E. A., Murray, L., Paukner, A. & Ferrari, P. F. (2014). The Mirror Neuron System as Revealed Through Neonatal Imitation: Presence from Birth, Predictive Power and Evidence of Plasticity. *Philosophical Transactions of the Royal Society. Series B Biological Sciences*, 369 (1644), 1–12.

Sorce, J. F., Emde, R. N., Campos, J. & Klinnert, M. D. (1985). Maternal Emotional Signaling: Its Effect on the Visual Cliff Behavior of 1-Year Olds. *Developmental Psychology*, 21 (1), 195–200.

Stein, B. E. & Meredith, M. Alex. (1993). *The Merging of the Senses*. Cambridge, MA: The MIT Press.

Stein, B. E., Stanford, T. R. & Rowland, B. A. (2014). Development of Multisensory Integration from the Perspective of the Individual Neuron. *Nature Reviews: Neuroscience*, 15 (8), 520–35.

Stern, D. N. (1985). *The Interpersonal World of the Infant: A View from Psychoanalysis and Developmental Psychology*. New York: Basic Books.

Suddendorf, T., Oostenbroek, J., Nielson, M. & Slaughter, V. (2013). Is Newborn Imitation Developmentally Homologous to Later Social-Cognitive Skills? *Developmental Psychobiology*, 55 (1), 52–58.

Tomkins, S. S. & McCarter, R. (1964). What and Where are the Primary Affects? Some Evidence for a Theory. *Perceptual and Motor Skills*, 18(1), 119–58.

Trevarthen, C. (1983). Emotions in Infancy: Regulators of Contacts and Relationships with Persons. In K. Scherer & P. Ekman, eds., *Approaches to Emotion*. Hillsdale: Lawrence Erlbaum, pp. 129–51.

Trevarthen, C. (1993). The Self Born in Intersubjectivity: The Psychology of an Infant Communicating. In U. Neisser, ed., *The Perceived Self: Ecological and Interpersonal Sources of Self-Knowledge*. Cambridge: Cambridge University Press, pp. 121–75.

Trevarthen, C., Kokkinaki, T. & Fiamenghi, Jr., G. A. (1999). What Infants' Imitations Communicate: With Mothers, With Fathers, and With Peers. In J. Nadel and G. Butterworth, eds., *Imitation in Infancy*. Cambridge: Cambridge University Press, pp. 127–85.

Van Baaren, R., Janssen, L., Chartrand, T. L. & Dijksterhuis, A. (2009). Where is the Love? The Social Aspects of Mimicry. *Philosophical Transactions of the Royal Society, Biological Sciences*, 364 (1528), 2381–89.

Vincini, S. (2020). "The Pairing Account of Infant Direct Social Perception. *Journal of Consciousness Studies*, 27 (1–2), 173–205.

Vincini, S. & Jhang, Y. (2018). Association but not Recognition: An Alternative Model for Differential Imitation from O to 2 Months. *Review of Philosophical Psychology*, 9, 395–427.

Vincini, S., Jhang, Y., Buder, E H. & Gallagher, S. (2017a). Neonatal Imitation: Theory, Experimental Design, and Significance for the Field of Social Cognition. *Frontiers in Psychology*, 8 (1323), 1–16.

Vincini, S., Jhang, Y., Buder, E. H. & Gallagher, S. (2017b). An Unsettled Debate: Key Empirical and Theoretical Questions are Still Open. *Behavioral and Brain Sciences* 40, 37–38, doi.org.10.1017. S0140525X16001977.

Welsh, T. (2006). Do Neonates Display Innate Self-Awareness? Why Neonatal Imitation Fails to Provide Sufficient Ground for Innate Self- and Other-Awareness. *Philosophical Psychology*, 19 (2), 221–38.

Wicker, B., Keysers,. C., Plailly, J. et al. (2003). Both of Us Disgusted in *My* Insula: The Common Neural Basis of Seeing and Feeling Disgust. *Neuron*, 40 (3), 655–64.

Williams, M. (1999). *Wittgenstein, Mind and Meaning: Towards a Social Conception of Mind*. London and New York: Routledge.

Zahavi, D. (2002). First-Person Thoughts and Embodied Self-Awareness: Some Reflections on the Relation Between Recent Analytic Philosophy and Phenomenology. *Phenomenology and the Cognitive Sciences*, 1, 7–26.

Zahavi, D. (2004). Phenomenology and the Project of Naturalization. *Phenomenology and the Cognitive Sciences*, 3, 331–47.

Zahavi, D. (2008). *Subjectivity and Selfhood: Investigating the First-Person Perspective*. Cambridge, MA: The MIT Press.

Zahavi, D. (2011). The Experiential Self: Objections and Clarifications. In M. Siderits, E. Thompson, and D. Zahavi, eds., *Self or No Self? Perspectives from Analytical, Phenomenological, and Indian Traditions*. Oxford: Oxford University Press, pp. 56–76.

Zahavi, D. (2013). Mindedness, Mindlessness, and First-Person Authority. In J. Schear, ed., *Mind, Reasons, and Being-in-the-World: The McDowell-Dreyfus Debate*. London and New York: Routledge, pp. 320–43.

Zahavi, D. (2014). *Self and Other: Exploring Subjectivity, Empathy, and Shame*. Oxford: Oxford University Press.

Zahavi, D. (2018). "Consciousness, Self-Consciousness, Selfhood: A Reply to Some Critics. *Review of Philosophical Psychology*, 9, 703–18.

Zwan, R. A., Etz, A., Lucase, R. E. & Donellan, M. B. (2018). Making Replication Mainstream. *Behavioral and Brain Sciences*, 41, 1–61.

Acknowledgments

My thanks to Alan J. Fridlund, Michael Fried, and Robert Pippin for their helpful comments on this project at various stages in its development. My thanks also to Susan Jones for responding to certain queries at an early moment in my research. I am also grateful to Jan Plamper for his commitment to the project and for encouraging me to publish it in this Cambridge Elements series. It gives me great pleasure to dedicate *Newborn Imitation: The Stakes of a Controversy* to Alan J. Fridlund, with heartfelt thanks for his many insights and constructive discussions over the years.

Cambridge Elements

Histories of Emotions and the Senses

About the Series

Born of the emotional and sensory "turns," Elements in Histories of Emotions and the Senses move one of the fastest-growing interdisciplinary fields forward. The series is aimed at scholars across the humanities, social sciences, and life sciences, embracing insights from a diverse range of disciplines, from neuroscience to art history and economics. Chronologically and regionally broad, encompassing global, transnational, and deep history, it concerns such topics as affect theory, intersensoriality, embodiment, human-animal relations, and distributed cognition.

Cambridge Elements

Histories of Emotions and the Senses

Elements in the Series

The Evolution of Affect Theory: The Humanities, the Sciences, and the Study of Power
Donovan O. Schaefer

Satire and the Public Emotions
Robert Phiddian

Newborn Imitation: The Stakes of a Controversy
Ruth Leys

A full series listing is available at: www.cambridge.org/EHES

Printed in the United States
By Bookmasters